A-LEVEL YEAR 1 SOCIOLOGY FOR O

UNIT 2A (Research Methods & Researching Social Inequalities)

SOCIOLOGY 2A STUDY GUIDE

Published independently by Tinderspark Press
© Jonathan Rowe 2022
www.psychologywizard.net
www.philosophydungeon.weebly.com

Visit the **Sociology Robot** YouTube channel

CONTENTS

ABOUT THIS BOOK

This book offers advice for teachers and students approaching OCR A-Level Sociology, **Paper 2 Section A (Research methods & researching social inequalities)**.

Study Guides for **Paper 2B (Understanding social inequalities)** and **Paper 3** follow.

Paper 2 Section A

This covers about a third of **Paper 2** in OCR Sociology. There are 4 questions worth 45 marks out of the 105 marks for the entire paper. It should take candidates just under an hour to complete this section.

Perspectives

In Paper 1, students learned about 3 vitally important sociological Perspectives: **Functionalism**, **Marxism** and **Feminism**. **Interactionism** was introduced later to make a fourth. Other Perspectives like **Postmodernism** and the **New Right** were introduced in **1B (Options)**.

Research methodology introduces two new methodological Perspectives that ties in with the theoretical Perspectives above: **Positivism** and **Interpretivism**. Understanding these debates about methodology will throw new light on Functionalism, Marxism and Feminism and help students to evaluate them deeply.

Studies

Sociological 'studies' (for A-Level purposes) are often papers published in academic journals, but are sometimes magazine articles, pamphlets produced by charities or activists or popular books.

Where texts are particularly famous or influential, I offer their titles, but candidates are not expected to know the titles of studies in the exam. All the studies referenced in this Study Guide are brought together at the end in a revision aid (p92).

The research methodology in this Study Guide is meant to be applied to research studies but isn't taken directly from them. But examples help. I start off using examples of studies from **1A: Socialisation, Culture & Identity** – notably Bourdieu's survey on taste, Parson's overview of gender roles in the American family and Willis' observation of working-class schoolboys. Later, new studies are introduced: these will all feature **in 2B: Understanding Social Inequalities** and are identified with * in the text.

I hope that encountering studies as methodology examples that they will meet again as research into inequality will help students revise and analyse these studies successfully.

REEARCH METHODS & RESEARCHING SOCIAL INEQUALITIES: CONTENT

What's this topic about?

In Paper 1, students were introduced to the main theoretical Perspectives in Sociology and some of the answers it proposes to questions about society. You learned dozens of 'studies' which are the results of investigating social behaviour in different settings. Now you will learn about METHODOLOGY which is how sociological research is actually carried out.

This should help you answer some important questions:

- What is the best way to investigate social phenomena? Is there a best way at all, or are all the ways flawed in some respect?

- Can sociologists be truly detached while they are investigating the society they live in? Should they even try to be detached?

- What are the limits of sociological investigation? Are some topics 'off limits' and are some ways of going about things dangerous, harmful or unfair?

Methodology

Methodology refers to the entire question of how to go about investigating society. It includes rather philosophical questions like what aspect of society should be investigated in the first place, practical questions like who should fund the research and who should carry it out, technical issues of where to do the research and how long for as well as ethical questions about how everyone involved should be treated during and after the research.

'Procedure' is another word that has a similar meaning to methodology, but 'procedure' is normally a narrower concern with the technical questions of where the research is done, who is involved, how long it lasts and what equipment is used. 'Methodology' is a wider term, taking in the issues of funding the research, publishing it, using it to influence social policy and making sure no groups are harmed or mistreated.

In **1A: Socialisation, Culture & Identity** students learned about evaluating sociological research. This often involves spotting the Perspective it comes from and discussing how rival Perspectives would criticise it. Methodology works as a powerful evaluative tool: as well as criticizing the theoretical basis of research, you can criticize or praise its methodology, arguing that it was carried out badly or well.

These methodological critiques don't just apply to the research on inequality you will meet in **2B: Understanding Social Inequalities**. When you revise the research from **Paper 1**, you should add methodological critiques to the studies there too.

CHAPTER ONE – THEORY & METHODS

Sociology tries to study society, which immediately raises the question, *How can you do that?* There are two main approaches or perspectives. One is to **imitate the way the natural sciences study the physical world** and treat social behaviour as the same sort of thing that plants or chemicals do in the lab. The other way is to **use imagination and empathy to 'put yourself in someone else's shoes'** and understand social behaviour from the inside. Neither approach is wrong, but they can lead to very different conclusions.

PERSPECTIVES

In **1A: Socialisation, Culture & Identity** you learned about the sociological perspectives based on Consensus (Functionalism) and Conflict (Marxism and Feminism) as well as the Social Action perspective (Interactionism). This section of the exam introduces methodological perspectives that direct sociologists to research things in different ways: the scientific **Positivist** approach and the more sensitive and imaginative **Interpretivist** approach (which is sometimes called Anti-Positivism).

These perspectives link together in interesting ways. **Functionalism** is usually Positivist in its approach as is traditional Marxist sociology. **Interactionism** is Interpretivist. **Feminism** and versions of modern **Neo-Marxism** often employ both methodological perspectives.

POSITIVISM

Positivism is a scientific approach. The word positivism comes from the philosophical idea that we only know things if they enter our mind through experience. This linked idea of truth being based on physical evidence experienced through the five senses is called **empiricism**. Empirical evidence is evidence that can be seen or heard or touched and empiricism is the basis for scientific proof. Empiricism is a very old idea but 'Positivism' was coined by **Auguste Comte** in the 19th century to mean the belief that society itself should be studied through physical evidence.

Emile Durkheim added to Positivism another idea: there are **social facts** which can be identified through scientific study of human behaviour and which have a *"coercive control"* over the way people act. For example, Durkheim thought that life in a big industrial city was a social fact that drove people to suicide.

For Positivists, the point of sociological research is to identify these social facts and explain the influence they have on people. This explanation takes the form of a scientific law that says that if there are certain social conditions then particular social outcomes must inevitably follow. Positivists hope that these social laws will predict upheavals in society (like riots, wars or revolutions) or social trends (such as marriages breaking up, crime waves or drug addiction).

In order to formulate these 'laws of society,' Positivists need to gather a lot of data (information) about social behaviour. This data needs to be **quantitative** (in number form) so that it can be statistically analysed. It needs to be gathered in a scientific way so that the researcher's personal biases or expectations don't influence the results. This impersonal approach is called **objectivity**.

AO2 ILLUSTRATION: DOCTOR WHO AND YOUTH CRIME

In November 2021, Conservative MP **Nick Fletcher** linked the casting of a female Doctor Who in the BBC's science fiction series to crime rates among young men. His remarks were widely mocked but they do illustrate the idea of social facts.

Fletcher complained that *"every male character or good role model"* is being given *"a female replacement,"* using examples like *Doctor Who* and *Ghostbusters*. Fletcher warned that young males would be left only antisocial role models like gangsters who *"make crime look cool"* and this would lead to *"young men committing crime."*

Role models are **social facts**: they influence you to imitate them. If you take away positive role models, it follows that people will stop imitating their behaviour. Fletcher's thinking is typically Positivist. However, it is not really based on lots of data gathered impersonally – in fact, it's based on a few anecdotes, which is the *opposite* of the Positivist approach. Nonetheless, Functionalists would accept Fletcher's broad hypothesis about how role models affect people; scientific research is needed to discover whether there are *in fact* fewer positive role models for young males (there are still a great many out there) and whether crime rates are *in fact* increasing among that group.

Other sociologists adopt the same Positivist perspective at times. It is common for Feminists to argue that violent pornography encourages crimes against women and to support this with detailed statistics about the consumption of pornography and the reporting of sexual assaults. Marxists also link increasing poverty or heavy-handed policing to rises in crime or riots. Both approaches identify social facts and support the link to social behaviour with statistical evidence.

Quantitative Data

Quantitative data means data in the form of numbers. Numerical data is much more impersonal and **objective** than words or descriptions: it's harder to misinterpret and it's less susceptible to being distorted by wishful thinking or prejudice.

Quantitative data can be expressed in **tables and graphs** which are easy to understand. Quantitative data allows for detailed comparisons of different groups and identifying trends. Quantitative data can also be used to show that *apparent* differences and trends don't really exist and that they only seem to be going on because people are focusing on a few high-profile examples (perhaps like Nick Fletcher MP, above).

Quantitative data is gathered from **structured observations** (p59), **structured interviews** (p58) and **closed questions in questionnaires** (p56).

However, quantitative data has its limitations. It can be very shallow and uninformative. It doesn't reveal feelings or motives. It is not very good for exploring individual cases or one-off events that don't reveal a pattern or a trend. Moreover, there is an old proverb that *"you can prove anything with statistics"* and numbers can easily be manipulated to support unreasonable conclusions.

AO2 ILLUSTRATION: THE BORIS BREXIT BUS

During the **2016 European Union (EU) Referendum**, the Brexit-supporting politician (and later Prime Minister) Boris Johnson organised a publicity stunt: a London bus with this message on the side:

"We send the EU £350 million a week. Let's fund the NHS instead."

Critics complained that this statistic was misleading. The figure was arrived at by taking the yearly amount the UK paid into the EU and dividing it by 52 to get a weekly figure. However, the UK also claimed a rebate back from the EU, so the real figure would have been £250 million or less. Moreover, a lot of extra costs would be incurred by leaving the EU, so the true figure was probably £130 million. Finally, even if there were savings, how could we be sure they would be paid into the NHS rather than (say) tax cuts?

Nonetheless, the figure of "£350 million" seems to have influenced voters. Like a lot of quantitative data, it's simple and memorable. An **Ipsos Mori survey (2018)** showed that 42% of people still believed the claim to be true. The **UK Statistics Authority** complained that the claim was *"misleading and undermines trust in official statistics."*

The controversy over the statistics on the Brexit Bus (source: FullFact.org)

Patterns & Trends

A great strength of Positivism is its focus on statistical patterns and trends in society. These could include rises in certain times of crime, changes in the gap between the rich and the poor or the number of women or people from ethnic minorities in top jobs.

The patterns and trends are important because Positivism is a **macro perspective** ('macro' means 'on a large scale'): it looks at society as a whole rather than individual actions and it tries to detect the social facts that are influencing people in general.

This macro perspective is sometimes called **structuralism**: the idea that society's structures dictate how people behave. It leaves very little room for **freewill or individual choice**. Functionalism and Marxism view people as shaped by their upbringing (primary socialisation) or social class. Feminism has a structuralist side to it as well, since it views Patriarchy in society as influencing people's attitudes and behaviour.

AO2 ILLUSTRATION: THE IMPACT OF CHRISTMAS ADVERTS

If you think it is unlikely that your individual behaviour could be influenced by social structures, consider Christmas adverts on TV. In 2018, John Lewis spent £18 million on TV adverts featuring the pop star Elton John. The advert had 50 million views across social media; John Lewis expects to earn back 20 times what it invests in Christmas advertising (source: BBC, 2019). UK customers spend £30 billion during the three months leading up to Christmas. However, profits dropped by 56% for John Lewis in that year, so did their popular advert really influence customers to shop in their stores? The figures back up the structuralist view (Christmas advertising encourages us to spend) but also oppose it (we don't necessarily shop in the places whose adverts we enjoy).

*If you studied **Media** as an option in **Paper 1B (Option 2)**, you will know different theories of media influence that explain how people obey media messages but also resist them.*

Screen shot of the 2021 John Lewis Christmas advert: Nathan & Skye (fair use)

9

The opposite of the macro perspective is the **micro perspective** that examines individuals or small groups and focuses on choice and freewill. Macro- or structuralist sociology might be missing out on the distinctive feature of human behaviour by ignoring these things.

Objectivity & Value Freedom

A crucial aspect of scientific methodology is **objectivity**, which means being neutral and impersonal, free from bias and keeping your opinions and preferences (or fears) out of the research process. It is not always easy to be objective when you are a scientist studying rocks, fossils or comets, because you might be excited by a new discovery or concerned that evidence doesn't back up your theory. It's even harder to be objective when studying people, especially when you focus on sensitive social issues (like racism, sexual assault, child abuse or poverty).

Positivists try to remain objective by following **standardised procedures**: they work out how their research will proceed beforehand and stick to that plan, ignoring interesting or concerning developments along the way. This leads to them favouring **structured observations** (p59), **structured interviews** (p58) and **closed questions in questionnaires** (p56). Objectivity is also achieved by inviting other sociologists to **replicate** your methodology to see if they come up with the same results. This is part of the **peer review process** in scientific research.

Positivists also pursue **value-freedom**, which means research that is free from values, opinions or interpretations. A value-free researcher shows no personal interest in the people being studied and has no preference for one outcome over another. Positivists use **sampling techniques** (p43) to make sure they are neutral towards their research participants, and they try to study society 'from the outside' as if they are not themselves a part of it. Critics argue that this sort of neutrality is impossible and that supposedly scientific research has values running through it.

AO2 ILLUSTRATION: DECOLONISING MATHEMATICS

Most people consider mathematics to be the most **objective** type of human thought and it is central to Positivism (the importance of **quantitative data** to identify **patterns and trends**).

However, critics argue that mathematics is **not value-free**. Mathematics is linked to the superiority of European civilisation and masculine thinking – the most famous mathematicians are males and the symbols used are Greek and Latin. Most people don't know about the huge contribution made to mathematics by Arabs (who gave us algebra, an Arabic word), ancient Egypt (fractions), India (which gave us the concept of zero) and of China. The Lebombo bone, discovered in South Africa, is the oldest known mathematical tool and it dates back to 35,000 BCE. These critics claim that mathematics must be **decolonised**, which means removing all of its associations with white, male, European superiority. Until then, mathematics will contain hidden but influential biases against other groups and cultures.

*When you study **2B: Understanding Social Inequalities** you will learn more about **Critical Race Theory (CRT)** and the project to **decolonialise** society.*

Positive Views of Positivism

Sounds a bit silly, doesn't it?

Positivism tries to make Sociology as scientific as possible. This means carrying out research on **large samples**, gathering detailed **quantitative data for statistical analysis** and following standardised procedures that can be **replicated by other researchers**. This sort of research is very **reliable** (p20).

Positivist research claims to **investigate social facts** and uses them to **formulate scientific laws** about how society operates. Positivism explores **patterns and trends** in populations and makes **predictions** about where these trends are heading and what will happen if changes occur in society.

Perhaps the most important advantage of 'scientific Sociology' is the **status** attached to science. Scientific research is viewed as more credible, it is taken more seriously and it reaches a wider audience than other types of research. It is more likely to inform **social policy** (p39) when governments act on it. This is particularly important for Perspectives that want to change society through research, such as **Feminists**, **Marxists** and the **New Right**. These perspectives are known as **structuralist** for their belief that the structures of society are more important than individual decision-making.

Negative Views of Positivism

Critics argue that society isn't the sort of thing that can be studied scientifically.

The Positivist focus on statistics and large samples ignores the importance of individual experiences, choices and **freewill**. Positivism views people as **puppets controlled by society**, but people are also the creators and shapers of social forces. Positivism ignores the impact of beliefs and the power of charismatic individuals or strongly motivated groups to change the course of history. In contrast, **Social Action** perspectives focus on exactly these subjects.

The Positivist focus on objectivity and value-freedom is criticised by **Interpretivists** (p13) who claim it is **not possible to be neutral** about your own society. They argue that researchers always smuggle their own assumptions and prejudices into their research, making it **biased**. These biases might be expressed in the samples selected, the wording of questions in surveys, the choice of topics to investigate or the way that conclusions are drawn from the data. For example, Feminists point out that mainstream Sociology is actually **'male-stream' Sociology** – it is from a male point of view, reflects male interests and ignores female experiences.

Other sociologists argue that the focus on science reflects Western cultural biases. This is linked to the **Postmodernist** argument that science is not really a way of discovering truth through reason and evidence, but instead is just another '**meta-narrative**' like a religion or a cultural belief. If this is the case, then the Positivist claim to investigate social facts is mistaken and Positivism just offers a *view* of society from a Western cultural standpoint.

Historic Positivists: Auguste Comte & Emile Durkheim

The 19th century French philosopher **Auguste Comte (1798-1857)** is sometimes called 'the Father of Sociology' and it was he who coined the terms 'Positivism' and 'Sociology.' For Comte, Positivism was more than just a research method: it was a political project. Comte believed that his Positivist outlook would replace religion and he called Sociology *'the Queen of the Sciences'* because he thought it would enable people to build a perfect society.

Emile Durkheim (1858-1917) was born a year after Comte died but carried on his commitment to a scientific understanding of society, although he rejected Comte's political project. Durkheim believed that Positivism could predict changes in society such as unemployment or unrest. Durkheim championed the **Comparative Method** which involves comparing groups and looking relationships between different variables. Durkheim's famous book *Suicide* **(1897)** used detailed statistical analysis of suicide rates all over Europe to link suicide to social facts like the type of religion and marital status. Durkheim concluded that suicide was more common when people lived individualistic and stressful lives without social support, such as in big industrial cities, after divorce and where Protestant (as opposed to Catholic) Christian religion was dominant.

Contemporary Positivist: Charles Murray

You were introduced to **Charles Murray**'s ideas about the Underclass in **1A: Socialisation, Culture & Identity** and will explore them in more detail in **2B: Understanding Inequality** as part of learning about the **New Right** perspective.

Murray's book *Losing Ground* **(1984)** analyses trends in the rise of crime in the USA since the 1960s and compares them for trends in unemployment and in the births of children outside marriage. This is similar to Durkheim's Comparative Method. He finds no match between the patterns of crime and unemployment but he does find a match between crime and the decline of marriage. Murray claims to have identified what Durkheim would call a **social fact**: boys born to unmarried mothers grow up to be *"essentially barbarians"* who turn to drugs and crime.

Murray identifies a sort of social law that says that people are kept honest and responsible by the need to work hard to support themselves and their family. If they do not need to do this – because, for example, the state supports men when they are unemployed and supports unmarried mothers – then people do not develop a sense of responsibility. Murray paints the picture of an 'underclass' that does little or no paid work, survives on benefits and petty crime and has no sense of sexual restraint or responsibility.

Murray is accused of being selective about what statistics he makes use of in order to exaggerate a social problem. This is the same as the criticism that Positivists *claim* to be neutral scientists stating the facts but are really human beings expressing their biased point of view in scientific language.

INTERPRETIVISM

Interpretivism (or **Anti-Positivism**) rejects the idea of 'scientific Sociology' because it focuses on the aspects of human life that are not suitable for scientific study: the interior world of beliefs, motives and choices. It is also sceptical about the possibility of studying society in a scientific way even if you do focus on observable behaviour because it argues that the sociological researcher can never be truly neutral as scientific research requires.

The founding figure of Interpretivism is **Max Weber** (p18), who rejected Positivism as a way of studying society. Weber pioneered the **Social Action** approach to Sociology, which developed into the **Interactionist** perspective that you learned about in **1A: Socialisation, Culture & Identity**.

Instead of searching for social facts and formulating sociological laws, Interpretivists place importance on how people make sense of their **social world**, how they **negotiate** the social pressures that try to coerce and control them and the different ways they show **agency** (self-direction and choice) in their lives. Rather than large samples, they often focus on **individuals** or on **small groups** through the sociological method of **ethnography** (p61). Interpretivists try to understand the **meaning** of social behaviour rather than trying to predict or control it.

Relativity by M C Escher (1953): going up or down? it depends on your point of view

Meanings & Experiences

Weber argues that what makes behaviour 'social' is the **meaning** people give to it. For example, the difference between a brawl and a boxing match is the way the fighters and the audience interpret what is going on. Another example might be family: this is not just a biological connection between people, it is the way people interpret their relationships to each other and how they think they are supposed to treat each other; some people who are not biologically related (such as stepchildren) are considered 'family' and some people who are biologically related (such as distant cousins) might not be considered 'family.'

Interpretivism claims that in order to make sense of the social world we have to understand how people **experience** it. A single social interaction might mean different things to the people involved, depending on the beliefs they hold and the social world they inhabit. There is no single objective fact behind any social behaviour, just multiple possible interpretations. This makes it impossible to study social behaviour scientifically; sensitivity is required (*c.f. **verstehen**,* p15).

AO2 ILLUSTRATION: AZEEM RAFIQ & YORKSHIRE CRICKET CLUB

Trigger warning: the repetition of an ethnic slur is used to illustrate this point.

Azeem Rafiq is a Pakistani-born cricketer who moved to the UK at age 10 and played for the prestigious Yorkshire County Cricket Club 2008-18, becoming captain in 2012. However, in 2020 he complained of racism in the club, in particular use of the racist slur 'Paki' (henceforth 'P-word'). The Club investigated but no one was disciplined and the use of the P-word was excused as *"friendly and good-natured banter."* Rafiq went public with his complaints and in the wider scandal the chairman of the Club resigned.

Rafiq's experience shows the importance of Interpretivist approaches. Some members of the Club regarded the P-word as 'banter' rather than racism; for Rafiq, this was a slur against his ethnicity and **not** a shortened form of his country of origin. Rafiq **experienced** racist abuse because the social interaction had a racist **meaning** for him (and would have that meaning for almost **all** British Asians). Marxists refer to this sort of language as **hegemonic discourse**: it reinforces **White privilege** by reminding non-Whites of their inferior status. Even when people use such slurs out of ignorance rather than malice, they support inequality with their language.

Second Test, Headingley (image by It's No Game)

Verstehen, Empathy & Rapport

Empathy is using your imagination to experience what another person experiences, to share their feelings and point of view. **Rapport** is a type of relationship characterised by trust, intimacy and easy communication. Both are important for an Interpretivist who tries to 'get inside another person's head' and see their **social world** as they see it.

Max Weber uses the word German word '***verstehen***' to describe Interpretivist methodology. '*Verstehen*' means 'understanding' and it involves having empathy with your research subjects and establishing a rapport with them. *Verstehen* is the opposite of the patterns and trends that Positivists focus on: it is personal insight rather than a statistical generalisation.

Subjectivity

Positivists aim to be objective (impersonal, neutral) but Interpretivists embrace the opposite of objectivity, which is **subjectivity**.

Subjectivity is often described as a bad thing: 'from your own subjective point of view' means you are not stepping back and viewing the situation in an unbiased way. However, Interpretivists claim that subjective experiences are valuable because they offer a **valid** insight into people's feelings. They also argue that the sort of objectivity Positivists aim for is in fact impossible: every view on any social situation is somewhat subjective. Instead of resisting subjectivity, it is better to embrace it and benefit from the insights you gain into **meanings and experiences** this way. This authenticity makes research more **valid** (p19).

AO2 ILLUSTRATION: OPRAH INTERVIEWS MEGHAN MARKLE

Oprah With Meghan & Harry was a 2021 TV show in which **Oprah Winfrey** interviewed the Duchess of Sussex and Prince Harry. During the interview, the Duchess talked about her experiences of mental ill health due to the racism of the Royal Family and the British news media.

Oprah Winfrey is a close friend and neighbour of Meghan Markle, so a **rapport** was quickly established. When Meghan revealed racist remarks has been made about her baby, Oprah gasped in horror, showing **empathy**. Oprah used the phrase '*speaking your truth*' to describe Meghan's account: the idea of '*your truth*' (rather than '*the* truth') draws attention to the **subjectivity** of Meghan's responses, which were the truth *as she saw it*.

The Queen later responded to the interview by saying "*Recollections may vary*" – in other words, her subjective experiences were different from Meghan's.

Critics complained that Oprah had not challenged any of the Duke and Duchess' claims and the British news media later exposed mistakes in their account. However, produced a fascinating insight into *one person's* experience of life in the Royal Family.

Researcher Imposition & Reflexivity

Researcher imposition is when the researcher imposes her own views, beliefs, prejudices or anxieties onto the research. This can be done through the **choice of topic to research** (such as Marxists focusing on class), **choice of sample** (such as young people or people from a particular neighbourhood) and even **choice of method** (such as choosing to interview people because you believe they would be too uneducated to complete a questionnaire). During the research, imposition can occur due to asking **leading questions** or guiding the participants' behaviour through **body language or non-verbal communication**.

Some research methods particularly beloved of Interpretivists, such as the **participant observation** (p60), are particularly prone to researcher imposition: you can change the behaviour of a small social group just by joining it. Studying motives and beliefs runs the risk that you project your own ideas onto your research subjects rather than discover their ideas.

One solution used by Interpretivists is **Reflexivity**. This is the process of reflecting on how you are influencing your own research. It includes acknowledging your own bias and the values and how they affect your findings. Reflexivity can be of various levels of depth and complexity:

- On a simple level, considering to what extent respondents are telling you what you want to hear – or feel inhibited from telling the truth or acting naturally in your presence or in the situation you set up. **Respondent validation** (p34) can be a solution to this problem.
- A more complex type of reflexivity is considering how your culture, gender, class or privileges might be influencing your research.
- The most complex type of reflexivity involves reflecting on your own theoretical bias, such as a Marxist focus on class at the expense of race or a Feminist focus on biological women at the expense of Trans and non-binary people.

AO2 ILLUSTRATION: KATE CLANCY'S REFLEXIVE MEMOIRS

Some Kids I Taught & What They Taught Me (2019) by Kate Clancy is an award-winning book of memoirs (an autobiography looking back on personal experiences). It is based on her career teaching disadvantaged children. However, the book was attacked on Twitter for containing discriminatory descriptions, such as referring to a Black pupil with *"chocolate coloured skin"* or two children with autism being *"jarring company."*

Clancy initially defended her writing then apologised for *"overreacting"* to criticism and said she was *"grateful"* for a chance to rewrite the book: *"I know I got many things wrong, and welcome the chance to write better, more lovingly."*

Some critics were dismayed that an author had been bullied into rewriting her own memoirs by anonymous Twitter-users. However, Clancy's decision resembles **reflexivity** in Sociology: she reflects on how her ethnicity and other privileges (as a person without learning disabilities) have led to her supporting harmful stereotypes and she adjusts her writing based on this insight.

Qualitative Data

Qualitative data means data in the form of words. Linguistic data is much more personal and **subjective** than numbers and statistics; it's more insightful and closer to the real-life experiences of actual people. Qualitative data can explore people's beliefs, feelings and motives. It is important for understanding one-off events (like being involved in a disaster) or exploring the perspective of minority groups whose experiences get 'drowned out' in large-scale patterns and trends. It can help overcome some of the institutional biases in Sociology, such as the tendency to approach things from a White or male perspective.

Qualitative data is gathered from **unstructured observations** (p60) and **semi-structured interviews** (p58) as well as **open questions in questionnaires** (p56).

However, qualitative data has limitations. It cannot create graphs or statistical analyses, compare groups or reveal large scale **patterns and trends**. Its sheer **subjectivity** makes it **unreliable** (p20) and hard to generalise beyond the original research situation. Even if the researcher is **reflexive**, biases will be present; reflexivity itself can make the research longwinded and self-indulgent.

Positive Views of Interpretivism

Interpretivists argue that society isn't the sort of thing that can be studied scientifically. They believe that statistics offer a misleading view of human experience and they reject the Positivist idea that we are 'puppets' controlled by society. Instead, they focus on the impact of beliefs and the power of charismatic individuals or strongly motivated groups to change society.

Research: Learn about an important leader who changed history or an influential group or belief system that persuaded other people to go along with it: you could focus on the **Abolitionists** who campaigned against slavery or a famous reformer like **Gandhi** (1869-1948).

Interpretivism offers a way out of the Western and male-orientated biases in Sociology through **reflexivity**. Researchers can address their own biases while carrying out research and reflect on them in their analysis. This is an improvement on **Positivism**, where researchers believe that, since they are collecting **quantitative data**, they must automatically be **value-free**, while all the time smuggling in biases they aren't aware of. Interpretivism also links to **Postmodernism** since it rejects the idea of a single truth 'out there' that can be reached by the scientific method. It accepts that truth is always **subjective** and there might be many truths, not just one.

Interpretivism has led to the new sociological methodology of **ethnography** (p61).

Negative Views of Interpretivism

The Interpretivist focus on subjectivity and reflexivity is criticised by **Positivists** (p6) who claim it is **important to be neutral** and step back from social situations to understand them clearly. They argue that, as social scientists, researchers should try to present social behaviour as factually as possible and avoid all **bias**.

By refusing to make use of scientific methods, Interpretivism risks offering only anecdotes or opinions. This is thought-provoking but cannot be the basis of **social policies** or used to criticise social institutions, because it might be completely unrepresentative. Statistical **patterns and trends** are needed to conform whether the findings apply to society as a whole or are limited to just the individuals being studied.

Reflexivity is fine for making the researcher more self-aware and sensitive, but it takes a lot of time and it takes up a lot of space in the research report. **Johnson & Duberley (2003)** argue that reflexivity can lead to **paralysis**, with the researcher so obsessed with questioning their own assumptions that they feel unable to draw confident conclusions.

Historic Interpretivist: Max Weber (1818-1883)

Max Weber (1864-1920) is one of the 'Big Three' founding sociologists, along with Karl Marx and Emile Durkheim. In **1A: Socialisation, Culture & Identity** you were introduced to Weber as the founder of the **Social Action** perspective that gave us Interactionism; in **2B: Understanding Social Inequalities** you will learn about **Weberianism** and how his ideas apply to society.

Weber is also the founder of the **Interpretivist** perspective in sociological methods. He rejected the **Positivist** methodology of Comte and Durkheim (p12) and argued that society is influenced by people's beliefs and choices rather than people being simply the 'puppets' of social institutions. Weber argued that science is not able to capture all social phenomena or explain why all social phenomena occur. Positivists focus on objects (data) but Weber argues sociologists should focus on subjects (people).

The Protestant Ethic & the Spirit of Capitalism (1905) was Weber's book which argued that Capitalism itself came about from the religious beliefs of Protestant Christians – they valued hard work and self-denial and this led to them investing profits back into their businesses. Weber's theory shows how social change comes about from beliefs and this is best discovered through investigating **qualitative data** and using *verstehen* (understanding, p15) rather than analysing statistics.

Contemporary Interpretivist: J Maxwell Atkinson

Discovering Suicide (1968) was a book by **J Maxwell Atkinson**, an Interpretivist who criticises Durkheim's famous research into suicide rates (p12). Atkinson argues that the official statistics used by Durkheim give a misleading view of suicide rates because a death is only considered a suicide if it is *defined as suicide* by a medical coroner. The coroner is guided in this decision by evidence like a suicide note but, in the absence of this, by beliefs and social expectations. In Catholic communities (which regard suicide as a sin and shameful), a coroner is more likely to define a self-caused death as an accident. Therefore, suicide is **socially constructed** and it is beliefs and values, not **social facts**, that explain the different suicide rates in Europe. Quantitative data from official statistics does not necessarily reveal social facts as Positivists claim.

THEORY & METHODS: A TOOLKIT

Sociological methods can be evaluated in terms of the broad perspective they belong to: **Positivist** research (p6) tends to be highly scientific and representative but lacking in validity; **Interpretivist** research (p13) is full of insight and meaning but unreliable and hard to generalise from.

These specific evaluation issues are discussed below. The studies used as examples are those that feature in the study guide for **1A: Socialisation, Culture & Identity**. The methodological strengths and weaknesses raised here make great evaluation points for students answering the 20-mark question in **Paper 1 Section A**.

Revise: Go through the studies you learned about in **1B Options (Family, Youth or Media)**; identify whether they come from a **Positivist** or an **Interpretivist** perspective or from a combination; decide whether the are strong or weak in **validity** or **reliability**, whether their data is **representative** and whether their conclusions can be **generalised**.

VALIDITY

Validity means 'truth' or 'authenticity.' Valid research gives a true picture of social reality – of **social facts**, if you are a Positivist, or of the **social world**, if you are an Interpretivist. A valid research method will **measure or record what it claims to be measuring/record**. An invalid method will be recording something else instead.

The issue of validity is a particular problem for measuring crime. Official crime statistics *claim* to measure the number of crimes going on in the country but they *actually* measure the crimes that are reported to the police and recorded by the police. Lots of crimes never get reported or recorded. This makes official crime statistics low in validity.

Interpretivist research is usually high in validity, because it goes to the 'source' by recording individual people's personal experiences. **Positivist** research is often low in validity because it uses statistics which are more removed from direct personal experience.

Validity can be assessed by using **multiple methods** (p67), for example combining a Positivist methodology (like official statistics or postal surveys) and an Interpretivist one (like semi-structured interviews). If the results match up, then they have **concordant validity**.

Research also has more validity if the results are in line with the findings of previous research on the subject or with what would be predicted by well-established theories.

Respondent validation (p34) and **triangulation** (p66) are both techniques for assessing the validity of research.

Validity is lowered if the **sample** being studied is **unrepresentative** (p22) or if time has passed and social change has made the research **ungeneralisable** (p22) to modern life.

METHODS PROFILE: PARSONS (1959)

Talcott Parsons' *The Social Structure of the Family* (1959) is a classic Functionalist text on family structures, gender roles and primary socialisation. It argues that males are biologically fitted to be **instrumental role leaders** (earning money, exerting discipline) and women the **expressive role leaders** (showing compassion and caring for their family).

Parsons' conclusions have been attacked for lacking validity. They are based on broad statistical trends about the structure of American families in the 1950s, but Parsons never investigates whether men and women *want* to live that way or how they *feel* about it. Feminist **Betty Friedan** in *The Feminine Mystique* (1963) identifies a widespread unhappiness among American housewives that she calls *"the problem that has no name."* She argues women are trapped within unfulfilling roles.

Social change since the 1950s has further reduced the validity of Parsons' views: women in the USA and UK today are far more likely to work themselves or be the main breadwinner for their family, so Parsons no longer describes how lots of people live.

RELIABILITY

Reliability means 'consistency.' Reliable research gives the same picture of social reality every time it is carried out, assuming the situation being studied remains the same. A reliable research method will **produce results that do not vary too much**. An unreliable method will produce different results every time, even though nothing important has changed.

The issue of reliability is a particular problem for measuring beliefs and intentions, such as voting intentions. For example, polling about whether people in Scotland favour independence from the UK shows support going up and down all the time. Is this because people's views are actually changing or are their flaws in the interviews and questionnaires?

Interpretivist research is usually low in reliability, because it focuses on feelings and beliefs which are very changeable or looks at particular social situations which are hard to reproduce. **Positivist** research is often high in reliability because it uses statistics which are gathered in consistent ways according to fixed procedures.

Reliability can be assessed by using **multiple observers or scorers**, for example getting another researcher to investigate the same situation using the same instruments (e.g. the same questionnaire or the same observation schedule). If the results match up, then they have **inter-rater reliability**.

Pilot studies (p32) are used to assess reliability at the start of the research process.

Research also has more reliability if repeating the research produces the same results (or broadly similar ones). This is known as **stability** or **test-retest reliability**.

Reliability is lowered if the research involves **subjective judgments**, because the same situation can be handled differently on separate occasions. For example, an unstructured interview might question two similar people but end up getting very different data from them, because different questions were asked or the answers were interpreted in different ways.

Important: Just because a piece of research is reliable, it doesn't automatically make it valid. You could have a consistent procedure but still end up with a wildly mistaken view of society. However, if the research is unreliable then it will probably lack validity too. If your results are all over the place, then it's hard to tell which result (if any) is telling you the truth.

METHODS PROFILE: WILLIS (1977)

Paul Willis' *Learning To Labour* **(1977)** is a ground-breaking study that adopts Interpretivist methods to support **Marxist** (or more precisely, **Neo-Marxist**) theories.

Willis follows a group of 12 working class teenagers ('the Lads') from 'Hammertown Boys School' (a fictional name for a school in Birmingham) and later factory work over 2 years. He studies 'the Lads' through **unstructured observations** (p60) and **interviews** (p58) in real life settings (their classrooms and later their workplaces). The unfiltered and authentic opinions of the schoolboys make this research very **valid**.

Willis used a range of research methods which increases the **validity** of his research. However, the boys may have acted up in front of Willis and exaggerated their anti-school attitudes, especially since Willis' Marxist attitudes towards school might have influenced them.

A different researcher with a different manner might have prompted different behaviour from the boys, which makes it **unreliable**.

However, Willis' research was conducted over a two-year period. Willis argues that the boys could never have faked insincere opinions for that long. The sheer duration of the study makes the results **more reliable**, compared to studying people just once or for a short term 'snapshot' of their views and behaviour.

Modern rules about safeguarding would make it difficult or impossible for an adult researcher to study children this closely for this long, so Willis' research is unlikely to be repeated. This further lowers its **reliability**. However, Willis' general approach to studying the schoolboys pioneered **ethnography** (p61) in Marxist Sociology. Many researchers argue the problems with reliability are a price worth paying for the insights generated by this into the experience of working-class life.

REPRESENTATIVENESS

Representativeness refers to how typical the people or the situation being studied are. A representative group of participants will resemble the wider population in important ways. A representative situation is similar to many other social situations in ordinary life.

Representativeness is usually achieved through using a **sample** of the wider population (*c.f.* p43). A representative sample closely matches the **patterns** in the population as a whole.

Positivists focus on the importance of representativeness. They achieve representativeness by making sure there is a statistical similarity between the sample they study (and they usually study large samples) and the **patterns and trends** in society. The representativeness of the sample justifies Positivists' claims to identify **social facts** in their research.

Interpretivists often downplay the importance of representativeness – or the possibility of ever studying anything truly representative. They often focus on unusual groups or the uniqueness of each situation. From an Interpretivist viewpoint, the social world is ever-changing and essentially **subjective** (p15), so you cannot claim that a particular group is 'typical.' Interpretivists argue that imagination and *verstehen* (p15) are more important than statistical similarities.

METHODS PROFILE: BOURDIEU (1984)

Pierre Bourdieu's book *Distinction* **(1979)** developed his theory of **cultural capital** using data drawn from two surveys of popular taste in France. This emphasis on statistical data is very much in the Positivist tradition of **Marxism**. Bourdieu cooperated with the statistician **Salah Bouhedja**, who used correspondence analyses on the data from the 'Kodak survey' (1963) and the 'taste survey' (1967). These gathered data from 1217 respondents in Paris and in a rural French town; Bourdieu also followed the surveys up with face-to-face interviews.

The surveys were **representative** of the French population of the 1960s. However, they were less representative of other European countries (like the UK) and unrepresentative of non-European countries (like Japan). The surveys get **less representative** with the passage of time: they are now 60 years old and public tastes have changed considerably. If Bourdieu's data is not representative (or is no longer representative) then his conclusions might not be **generalisable** (*see below*) to other countries or France in the 21st century.

GENERALISABILITY

Generalisability is how a study's findings can be applied to wider society. It is related to **representativeness**: research with a representative sample or situation will have generalisable conclusions; an unrepresentative study will not have conclusions that can be generalised beyond the people or situations that were involved.

Malcolm Williams (2000) argues that there are three types of generalisability:

- **Total generalisations:** these are the sort of generalisations made in the physical sciences when situations are similar in every detail (such as the behaviour of electricity in a circuit); Williams argues that social sciences like Sociology cannot make this sort of generalisation because social situations are always unique.

- **Statistical generalisations:** these generalisations rest on a high degree of similarity between social situations and a probability that other social situations will resemble the one being studied; Williams argues that this is often used in science and is the basis for **representative sampling** (p22) used by Positivists.

- ***Moderatum* generalisations:** *moderatum* is Latin for 'restricted' and generalising *in moderatum* means arguing that **some** features of the situation being studied might apply to wider society; Williams argues this is the basis for the **subjective** research (p15) used by Interpretivists.

If research is ungeneralisable then its conclusions are not **valid** (p19) if they are applied to any group or situation other than the one that was studied.

METHODS PROFILE: MCINTOSH (1968)

Mary McIntosh wrote *The Homosexual Role* (1968) after conducting surveys and interviews with homosexual men in London and Leicester, especially in the Gateways club and the Gigolo Coffee Bar in Chelsea. These homosexual men cannot be **representative** of *all* homosexual men everywhere, nor of lesbians or bisexual people, and therefore McIntosh's conclusions **cannot be generalised** to other groups and situations.

However, McIntosh takes an **Interpretivist** approach, describing homosexuality as a social role that is constructed differently at other times and places. She argues that it is in fact **impossible to generalise** about homosexuality; she uses this argument to show that homosexuality should not be written off as deviant behaviour or a mental illness (as was common in the 1960s). McIntosh makes ***moderatum* generalisations** from her data, pointing to the way homosexual men who are exposed to a similar gay subculture tend to behave in similar ways, but men who are not exposed to that subculture do not.

McIntosh is another early pioneer of **ethnography** (p61) as a sociological method to understand the social world of marginalised subcultures.

EXAM PRACTICE: THEORY & METHODS

The OCR exam has four questions in **Paper 2 Section A**, based on two source items:

Source A

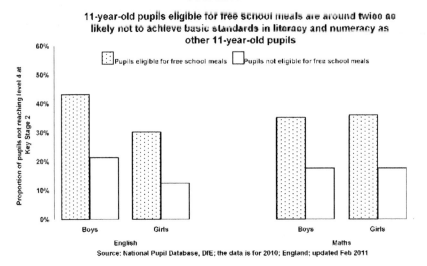

11-year-old pupils eligible for free school meals are around twice as likely not to achieve basic standards in literacy and numeracy as other 11-year-old pupils

Source: National Pupil Database, DfE; the data is for 2010; England; updated Feb 2011

Source B

Researchers investigated children's awareness of their social class and the limits it put on them in school. The children were aged eight to 13, some living on a disadvantaged housing estate and others attending a private school. The researchers carried out interviews to gather qualitative data. The more advantaged children described a much richer set of experiences in school, both inside the curriculum (i.e. in lessons and homework) and outside the curriculum (e.g. in clubs and societies). For the disadvantaged children, issues such as discipline and detention dominated the discussion.

Here is an extract from the interviews:

Interviewer: "Is life more unfair to some children than others?"
Girl (early secondary school) "Yes, it is. It's unfair for us because we have to just listen to teachers all the time."
Interviewer: "But isn't that the same for all children?"
Girl: "No. It's not, because if you're rich you get to go to a posh school where the teachers probably teach you with respect."

The children had developed clear stereotypes of 'chavs' and 'posh' children. These stereotypes were quite extreme, and the children always applied them to other children rather than describing themselves. The researchers believe this demonstrates an early awareness of social class differences. Negative attitudes were based on children lacking confidence in their own ability to do well within the system. The researchers conclude that if children had better opportunities and experiences, their attitudes to school would become more positive.

1. Summarise the data shown in **Source A**. **[4 marks: 4 AO2]**

*Make **two** points about the data. It is vital that you quote actual figures from the graph and draw conclusions from them (or you are not 'summarising' the data, only restating it). For example, about 43% of boys on FSM do not reach level 4 in English. In order to summarise, you need to say whether this is higher or lower than girls, Maths students or children **not** eligible for FSM.*

2. With reference to **Source B**, explain **two** reasons why sociologists might collect qualitative data. **[6 marks: 2 AO1 + 4 AO2]**

Write a couple of sentences about each reason. You might focus on high validity, subjectivity, or verstehen. You need to support each reason with an example from the source – a really good idea is to quote something from the source.

3. With reference to **Source A**, explain **one** advantage and **one** disadvantage of sociologists looking for patterns and trends in children's attainment at school. **[10 marks: 4 AO2 + 6 AO3]**

Write two short paragraphs, one about an advantage (such as revealing social facts, making predictions, generalising to other groups, objectivity, science) and one about a disadvantage (such as shallowness of statistics, lack of individual focus, possible subjective bias, lack of verstehen). You need to support each reason with an example from the source – a really good idea is to quote a number (or approximate number) from the graph.

4. Using **Source B** and your wider sociological knowledge, explain and evaluate using Interpretivist methods to study children's attitudes to education. **[25 marks: 5 AO1 + 5 AO2 + 15 AO3]**

*Write four paragraphs/arguments – two strengths and two weaknesses of Interpretivism would work well. Each paragraph should introduce a sociological idea with an example or comparison from **Source B**. Each paragraph should finish off with a developed evaluation (see **Chapter 4** for this). For example, you could write about Interpretivism allowing people to express their own views and drawing imaginative conclusions, but also how Interpretivist methods tend to be unreliable and can only be generalised in moderatum.*

In questions 2-3 you can pick up the AO1 marks from using sociological terminology and relating things to sociological debates (e.g. Positivism vs Interpretivism). Named sociologists and studies aren't particularly important, but **Comte**, **Durkheim** and **Weber** are relevant for questions 2-3.

Question 4 is a full essay in which you are invited to deploy *"your wider sociological knowledge"* so famous sociologists definitely belong in your answer and a comparison to **Willis'** study would also help.

CHAPTER TWO – THE RESEARCH PROCESS

Lots of people have opinions about society but they are mostly drawn from personal experience or anecdotes. Authors can use their imagination to explore society. Journalists report on events in society but with the purpose of entertainment (sensationalism) or serving the political agenda of their editor or boss. Sociology is different because it gathers **empirical** (observable) **data** to support its conclusions.

Steps in the research process are common to **Positivists** and **Interpretivists**. Studies are used as examples are all from **2B: Understanding Social Inequalities**.

CHOICE OF RESEARCH TOPIC

Sociologists choose topics to research: the effect of unemployment, changing attitudes to disability, discrimination against homosexuality, the rise or fall of national identity, the impact of different family types of children, to name a few.

Some sociologists pursue a **personal interest**. **Tom Shakespeare** studies disability at least in part because he is a wheelchair-user. **Mary McIntosh** (p23) is a lesbian, and her sexuality perhaps influences her interest in homosexual identities. Other sociologists choose topics inspired by their **sociological perspective**. **Paul Willis** (p21) is a Marxist and this perhaps explains his interest in the way working class children experience education.

Often the choice of topic is dictated by the **funding body** (*c.f.* p40). Sociology is a job and researchers must earn money. If they are not being funded by a university then sociological research is funded by governments, political parties, charities (such as the **Joseph Rowntree Foundation**) and media organisations (like the **BBC**). Researchers might be influenced in their choice of topic by the possibility of publishing a book or creating a documentary and this directs them towards topics of public interest (or current fashions or moral panics).

Finally, **new developments in society** attract research interest. Elections and referendums spark research into voting patterns; shocking crimes or terrorist attacks prompt research into deviancy; new technology (such as dating apps or driverless cars) invite research into the digital world; events like the national lockdowns during the 2020-21 Coronavirus Pandemic provide opportunities to study how people react to isolation and social distancing.

Interpretivists argue that the choice of topic is a value judgment and shows that research is never **value-free** as Positivists would insist. Interpretivists use **reflexivity** (p16) to reflect on their involvement in their own research, including their starting choice of topic.

Positivists aim to be **objective** (p10) in their research and claim that the choice of topic does not introduce significant biases into their work. However, even **Durkheim** (p12) might not be as objective as he claimed: Durkheim had a close friend, Victor Hommay, who committed suicide and this may have influenced his decision to research suicide for his 1897 book.

METHODS PROFILE: SEWELL ET AL.* (CRED, 2021)

The **Commission for Racial & Ethnic Disparities (CRED)** is a UK government body headed by **Tony Sewell**, an educationalist who has previously researched the under-attainment of Black boys in British schools. The **2021 CRED Report** is an independent investigation with the topic of structural racism in the UK. The Report's conclusions are very controversial.

The CRED Report is influenced by many factors. In 2020, protests occurred around the world under the banner of **'Black Lives Matter'** and the UK's Conservative Government promised to investigate allegations that UK society was structurally racist. In the aftermath of Brexit, the UK Government wanted to demonstrate that Britain had a bright future of equality and fairness and funded this research with that aim. Sewell and his commissioners have strong **Functionalist** principles that make them sceptical about conflict in society. It is possible that the CRED Report was commissioned specifically to disprove accusations of racist bias in British society.

This is an example of choice of topic being shaped by **new developments in society** (Black Lives Matter protests), the **funding body** (the UK Government) and **sociological perspective** (Functionalism). Critics complain that this **bias** right at the outset makes the Report's findings a foregone conclusion, despite a **Positivist** methodology that involved *"sifting through a mass of data, reading the evidence from experts and speaking to communities."*

BRITAIN'S RACE REVOLUTION

By **Daniel Martin**
Policy Editor

Landmark report says UK 'a model to world' on diversity – and finds NO evidence of institutional racism

BRITAIN is a model to the world of a successful multi-ethnic society, a major review concluded last night.

It found no evidence the UK is institutionally racist – in a rejection of the common view among activists.

The Commission on Race and Ethnic Disparities, set up by Boris Johnson in the wake of the Black Lives Matter protests, concluded that although Britain is not yet a 'post-racial society', its success should be a model for white-majority countries. Commission chairman

Tony Sewell said the UK had progressed into a 'successful multi-ethnic and multicultural community' which was a 'beacon to the rest of Europe and the world'. He warned ministers must also consider

the needs of the white working class, saying his report had uncovered how 'stuck' some groups were.

The landmark review found children from many ethnic minorities do as well

or better at school than white pupils, which was creating fairer and more diverse workplaces. It called on firms to phase out 'unconscious bias' training **Turn to Page 2**

Daily Mail headline, 31 March 2021: the Mail is a Conservative-supporting newspaper and approves of the CRED Report and its choice of topic

Research: read the Introduction to the 2021 CRED Report https://www.gov.uk/government/publications/the-report-of-the-commission-on-race-and-ethnic-disparities and then research criticisms of its findings

AIMS, HYPOTHESES & RESEARCH QUESTIONS

The Topic is a broad area for inquiry. **Aims** are what the research hopes to reveal about the topic.

- **Aims** can still be quite vague (like 'finding out more' about something) but a **research question** has to be more specific. The **2021 CRED Report** (p27) seems to address the research question: 'Is racism in the UK declining?' and it comes to the controversial conclusion, 'Yes it is.'

> **Revision:** go back over your notes on the Key Studies you have learned about so far; what seems to be the **research question** behind the main ones?

- A **hypothesis** is even more specific than a research question, because a hypothesis is a *prediction*. Researchers test the hypothesis by gathering data. If the evidence goes against (refutes) the hypothesis, then the researcher needs to make changes to the hypothesis and start over. However, if the evidence supports the hypothesis then the researcher can develop a **theory**.

- **Theories** are the boldest form of sociological thought: they are accounts of how society works for different groups of people. There are Marxist, Functionalist and Feminist theories. **Induction** is the process of using evidence to build a theory out of testing hypotheses. **Deduction** is the process of making predictions based on a theory.

Positivists think that Sociology should work like the physical sciences, by proposing strict hypotheses and testing them; they refer to their theories as **social facts**. They argue that induction is an effective way of constructing theories and deductions can be made from them.

Interpretivists think that Sociology cannot and should not work like the physical sciences. They argue that induction is *not* an effective way of constructing theories because no amount of induction can ever justify an overarching theory that covers new phenomenon. This is the '**problem of induction**' which often uses the example that no amount of observations of white swans can ever justify the theory that 'all swans are white.'

Interpretivists argue that researchers instead need to use **empathy** and *verstehen* (p15) to understand the **social world**.

Most sociologists pursue **a 'third way'** combining the scientific rigour of Positivism with the imagination and **reflexivity** (p16) of Interpretivism. They develop theories that are much more cautious than the physical sciences and do not claim to make confident deductions from them, but merely indicate possibilities that need to be explored further.

METHODS PROFILE: WILKINSON & PICKETT* (2009)

A controversial book in Sociology is **Herrnstein & Murray**'s *The Bell Curve* **(1994)** which argues that inequality in society is a product of people's innate intelligence (or lack of it). The authors conclude that inequality is a good thing (since the fear of poverty drives people to work hard) and cannot be 'fixed' by social policy.

A reply to *The Bell Curve* came from two UK researchers, **Richard Wilkinson & Kate Pickett** who wrote *The Spirit Level* **(2009)**. Wilkinson & Pickett's **aim** is to present a different view of inequality that is not unavoidable or beneficial, in the way *The Bell Curve* presented it.

Wilkinson & Pickett's **research question** is, *Are unequal societies less happy and healthy overall than more-equal ones*? They test this by measuring 11 different social problems (like drug abuse, obesity, teenage pregnancy, violence and lack of community trust) across different countries.

Wilkinson & Pickett's **hypothesis** is that these problems will increase with the amount of inequality in a country (whether there is a big gap in wealth), as opposed to whether the country is rich or poor overall.

They find that countries where there is a small gap between the rich and the poor (e.g. Scandinavian countries, Japan) suffer less from these problems, but countries where there is a large gap (e.g. the UK and the USA) do worse.

Wilkinson & Pickett build a **theory** from this: inequality makes people feel stressed and this in turn leads to things like smoking, overeating and violence which produces depression and anxiety. From this theory we can deduce that governments should try to reduce inequality in order to make the population happier and healthier.

The Spirit Level is a good example of **Positivist** research because it analyses huge samples using **statistics** to identify **patterns and trends** (p9). It points to social facts about inequality, health and happiness. It had a big effect on **social policy** (p39), with both Labour and Conservatives incorporating it into their manifesto policies during the 2010 General Election.

PRIMARY & SECONDARY DATA

Primary data is data that the researcher collects herself, specifically for the research she is doing. This data will be exactly what the researcher needs to test her hypothesis and the researcher can guarantee its **validity** (p19) and **reliability** (p20) since she collected it herself.

The main problem with primary data is time and trouble. Collecting evidence is **time consuming** and **expensive**. Gathering some sorts of data might even be **dangerous** or present **ethical problems** if you are researching children, criminals or the mentally ill.

Willis' study of 'the Lads' in *Learning To Labour* (1977, p21) is a good example or primary data and so is **McIntosh's 1968 research into homosexuals** (p23).

The alternative is to gather **secondary data**. This is data that has already been gathered by someone else. The researcher can take advantage of someone else's research by using the evidence they gathered. Obviously, there is much **less time and trouble** this way. The Internet makes it particularly easy to access secondary data.

The problem is that this data was gathered for different purposes and it might use **different categories** or **define concepts differently** (for example, defining social class or poverty). It might have biases or be invalid or unreliable. It might use an **unrepresentative sample** or be impossible to **generalise** (p22) to the situation the new researcher is interested in.

Bourdieu's use of mass surveys into French culture (p22) is a good example of using secondary data and so is **Wilkinson & Pickett**'s use of data on happiness, health and inequality (p29).

METHODS PROFILE: HECHT ET AL.* (2020)

Katharina Hecht and her colleagues carried out an analysis of social mobility in the UK since the 1970s. They used **secondary data**, taking statistics from a **longitudinal study** (p36) carried out by the **Office for National Statistics (ONS)** on people born in the 1950s, 1960s and 1970s.

Hecht analysed the ONS data by focusing on the **elite earners** (the top 1%) and calculates how many enjoyed **long-range mobility** (rising up from the lowest social class into the elite). She shows that those born in the 1950s had more long-range social mobility than those born later on.

The ONS data wasn't originally collected to study long-range mobility among elite earners. **Official statistics** like these won't include people who moved abroad or who were born abroad and arrived in the UK later. They won't include elite earners who hide their wealth (for example, criminals and 'tax-dodgers'). Secondary data is limited by whoever first collected it. However, Hecht would not have been able to gather such data going back so far on her own.

Hecht also collected **primary data** by interviewing 30 elite earners about how they viewed their success. This sort of **methodological pluralism** (p67) gets round some of the problems of data and also mixes **Positivist** and **Interpretivist** methodology by studying both statistics and what wealth actually means to people.

OPERATIONALISATION

Operationalisation means defining your concepts in a way that is clear and measurable. Vaguely defined concepts make research **unreliable** (because you might define things differently every time to come across them, sometimes recording them and sometimes ignoring them). Research concepts need to be operationalizable in order for another social scientist to **replicate** the methodology and see if they get the same results.

Usually, the **aim** of a study is not operationalised: it's a general statement of interest. The **research question** is more clearly defined and the **hypothesis** should be fully operationalised.

Concepts that sociologists need to operationalise include ethnicity and social class. Ethnicity needs to be operationalised so it's clear which ethnic group people fit into; for example, '**Black And Minority Ethnicity**' (**BAME**) can be a catch-all term for non-White people but many sociologists want to operationalise this more precisely, identifying whether people are Black-Caribbean or Black-African, for example. Similarly, there are several different scales for measuring social class and in **1A: Socialisation, Culture & Identity** you learned about the **Registrar General's Scale**, the **National Readership Survey Scale** and the new British Class Scale developed by **Savage et al. (2013)**.

Operationalisation is particularly important for **Positivists**, who want their research to be as scientific as possible. It is also important for **Interpretivists** who want to avoid the accusation they are too **subjective** (p15). However, some Interpretivists argue that it is operationalising concepts that actually smuggles biases into the research. For example, defining social class based on the job of the male in a household makes women less important in sociological research.

METHODS PROFILE: WILKINSON & PICKETT* (2009, cont'd)

The Spirit Level (2009) was introduced on p29. **Wilkinson & Pickett** try to **operationalise** a very vague concept: the health and happiness of a society. They focus on eleven social problems: physical health, mental health, drug abuse, education, imprisonment, obesity, social mobility, trust and community life, violence, teenage pregnancies and child wellbeing. They measure physical health by infant mortality rates, which is the proportion of newborn babies that die in their first year. This is a surprisingly high figure in the USA (7 per 1000), but low in Japan, Finland, Sweden and Norway (lower than 4).

Wilkinson & Pickett have been criticised for what they do *not* operationalise. For example, they do not include suicide as one of the measures of health and happiness. Finland has one of the highest suicide rates in the world (11.6 per 100,000 people; source: **OECD, 2005**).

This shows that operationalisation always involves including some things but leaving other things out. **Interpretivists** claim this is an example of **researcher imposition** (p16) that makes it impossible for research to be truly **value-free** (p10).

PILOT STUDIES

Once a study has a clearly operationalised hypothesis, it's necessary to test if it works. A **pilot study** is a 'test drive' for a research study, usually with a very **small group of participants**. The purpose is to flag up problems so that these can be corrected before the *real* research goes ahead.

Positivists use pilot studies to test that their procedures are **standardised and impartial**. At no point during the course of the study should the researcher be required to step in and make ad hoc 'fixes' to the way the study works, such as clarifying what questions mean, re-wording instructions or tweaking the list of things being observed. Once the study works without any extra input from the researcher, it's ready to be rolled out to a wider population.

Interpretivists are more likely to focus on **bias** in the way the study plays out, such as unquestioned assumptions in the questions coming to light, minority groups not being represented in the sample or the results reflecting prejudices. A pilot study is part of the ongoing process of **reflexivity** (p16) used by Interpretivists.

Positivists and Interpretivi51sts both use pilot studies to catch straightforward mistakes in the research design, especially things like **unrepresentative samples** (p22), inappropriate questions or **ethical issues** with the way participants are treated (p51).

The results of pilot studies usually don't get written up in the finished report, although Interpretivists might refer to them as part of reflexivity.

KEY STUDY: CORRELL* (2017)

One study that does refer to pilot studies is **Shelley Correll**'s "Small Wins Model" for removing bias from the recruitment and promotion of women in business. Correll and her team focus on educating managers and workers about bias, diagnosing where gender bias could enter business practices and developing tools that help reduce bias and inequality in a measurable way.

Correll carried out pilot studies over 3 years with medium sized tech companies around California, USA.

Image: Shelley Correll

As well as training managers in techniques to reduce workplace inequality, Correll's team listened to their feedback and made adjustments to the model. This is an example of **reflexivity** (p16) in research.

DATA COLLECTION

Data collection is also known as issues surrounding the **choice of methods**. The main issue here is theoretical: is the research guided by **Positivism** or **Interpretivism**?

- **Positivism** favours scientific forms of data collection that are **objective**, **value-free** and highly **replicable** in order to reveal **social facts**: large-scale **questionnaires** (p56), **structured interviews** (p58) and **observations** (p59), **official statistics** (p65), all gathering **quantitative data** (p7).

- **Interpretivism** favours gathering data in a more intimate and **subjective** way to explore the **meaning** of social behaviour: **ethnography** (p61), **participant observations** (p60), **unstructured interviews** (p58), all favouring **qualitative data** (p17).

Many researchers don't care about these theoretical disagreements and just use whatever methods are convenient. Some researchers deliberately try to pursue a **'third way'** between Positivism and Interpretivism, combining elements of both.

There are practical considerations, such as **time and cost**.

- **Expensive data collection** involves training researchers as interviewers or observers, recruiting large samples or hiring translators. **Time-consuming research** is expensive as well, since researchers have to be paid, so **longitudinal studies** (p36) cost a lot and don't yield results for months or years.

- **Cheap research** involves simple questionnaires or structured interviews with closed questions, structured observations and small samples; since sociologists are often based in university, this often means samples of university students. Official statistics can be obtained cheaply through the Internet. **Snapshot studies** can be carried out quickly so the costs don't spiral and the data is collected straight away. **Secondary data** (p30) reduces both time and costs.

Finally, there are issues of sensitivity in subject matter and social characteristics of researchers.

- **Sensitive subject matter** involves topics like racism, sexual or child abuse, studying the elderly or the mentally ill or where there is a danger of research causing offence or adding to the marginalisation of a group of people. These topics usually involve well-trained researchers approaching small groups of participants; time is needed to establish trust and **rapport** (p15). **Reflexivity** (p16) is important because the researcher needs to think carefully about their treatment of the research subjects.

- **Social characteristics** includes the researcher's ethnicity, gender, class and age. Sometimes it is important for the researchers to be similar to the research subjects (for example, female victims of sexual abuse should be interviewed by other women). Reflexivity encourages the researcher to reflect on how their characteristics might have caused the research subjects to feel inhibited, which lowers the validity of the study.

METHODS PROFILE: HECHT ET AL.* (2020, cont'd)

Katharina Hecht's study of social mobility since the 1970s is on p30. The study is a good example of a **'third way'** approach combining Positivist and Interpretivist styles of data collection.

Hecht's aim is to show that the UK is getting less socially mobile. She uses official statistics from the Office for National Statistics: this is **secondary data** (p30) that is cheap and quick to access and it reveals **patterns and trends** over the last 50 years.

However, Hecht also wants to explore how elite earners *feel* about the wealth and what social mobility *means* to them. To this end she uses a short questionnaire and semi-structured interviews with 30 elite earners to find out if they attribute their success to their own hard work or to their privileged backgrounds and whether they believe other people can reach their level.

Getting hold of very rich businesspeople and interviewing them about their wealth is difficult to arrange (unless you are yourself another very rich businessperson) and time consuming, so Hecht only collects data on 30 people, whereas the ONS data collects data on over 500,000 people. This illustrates the difference between **micro-** and **macro- level** data collection and the way they can be combined in a single study.

RESPONDENT VALIDATION

Pilot studies (p32) try to detect bias *before* the research is carried out in full. **Respondent validation** is a way of detecting bias afterwards. It involves getting the people who took part in the study (the 'respondents') to confirm (or 'validate') the researcher's interpretation of their views or behaviour. It is also known as participant validation or 'member checking' and it measures the **validity** of research (p19).

Respondent validation is an important part of the **reflexivity** (p16) practised by Interpretivists.

Respondent validation usually involves presenting your research participants with your findings before going on to publish them. Ideally, all the participants will study the findings and discuss them in an interview with the researcher. This gives the participants a chance to correct misunderstandings or disagree with conclusions (e.g. saying *'That's not what I meant...'* or *'You misunderstood what I was doing ...'*). This is particularly important for Interpretivists who want to get **insight** into the **social world** of their participants, but it might be used by Positivists who are trying to remain **value-free** (p10).

Alan Bryman (1988) points out problems with respondent validation:

1. Getting all the participants back together to comment on the research is **difficult and time-consuming**; often respondent validation only involves a few participants (a sample of a sample) to their views might not be **representative** of the other participants who didn't take part in the validation

2. Similarly, **interviews** (p58) might be inconvenient, so validation often involves **questionnaires** (p56) which can be misleading or off-putting
3. Sociological research is often written in **technical language** and involves difficult concepts. Unless they are educated in a particular way, respondents might struggle to understand the researcher's conclusions. In particular, they might interpret the research as criticising them.

METHODS PROFILE: JONES ET AL.* (2010) vs HECHT ET AL.* (2020)

Ian Jones, Miranda Leontowitsch & Paul Higgs interviewed 20 men and women who were top managers in the UK about their decisions to take early retirement. Their aim was to explore whether retirement was a positive or negative change in life.

The researchers refer to their participants as **quasi-subjects**. This is a term developed by **Ulrich Beck (2004)** to describe participants who *partly* represent an institution they belong to (such as their job, age group and social class in this case) but who *also* have freewill and individuality and can speak for themselves. This makes it important to investigate to what extent the participants are speaking as 'typical' members of their age group and social class and to what extent they are unique individuals with their own personal agenda.

Respondent validation is important in this example. For example, Jones et al. conclude that their quasi-subjects felt grateful and privileged to be able to take early retirement; they were aware that people in previous generations weren't able to do this and their own children and grandchildren might not be so fortunate either. This is the sort of conclusion that needs to be validated by the respondents themselves – and since the quasi-subjects were an educated group they were able to understand the researchers' aims and conclusions and confirm that this was indeed how they felt.

Katharina Hecht's study of social mobility since the 1970s is on p30. Hecht's aim is to show that the UK is getting less socially mobile. She interviews 30 elite earners who report that they earned their top positions by hard work and merit. However, Hecht contrasts their views with official statistics since the 1970s which tell another story: compared to people in the past, these elite earners started out with more advantages (wealthy parents, good education, etc). Hecht identifies the **'meritocratic paradox'** which is that, as society gets more unfair, the people who benefit believe it has treated them fairly.

However, Hecht's 30 participants would *not* agree with her conclusions. In Hecht's research, they are not quasi-subjects but simply **subjects**: they are treated as people who cannot see past their own circumstances to understand what's really going on. It's rather typical of **structuralist** (and especially **Marxist**) research to treat participants as subjects. Marxists often argue that people suffer from **'false consciousness'** that stops them from appreciating how unfair Capitalist society really is. False consciousness means that respondents often will not validate Marxist research.

LONGITUDINAL STUDIES

Most sociological research takes the form of **'snapshot' studies** that give a picture of social facts (for Positivists) or the social world (for Interpretivists) at a particular moment in time. Sometimes this is exactly what the researcher wants; for example, a researcher's aim might be to study people's reaction to a terrorist attack or a sporting victory or how crime rates change after a new law is brought in.

Often, these 'snapshots' are **unreliable**. Participants might be 'having a bad day' or there might be stress or changes going on in their lives that make their responses **ungeneralisable** (p22).

Image: Ryan McGilchrist, 2008

Longitudinal studies take place over a long period of time: usually weeks or months but sometimes years. The participants in a longitudinal study are known as a **cohort** and the researcher follows the cohort over time, measuring their attitudes, relationships or behaviours at regular intervals.

- A **prospective longitudinal study** identifies a cohort who share something in common (such as being born in the same year) and follows them over time as they age, observing changes that happen to them. The biggest problem with this is **sample attrition**, which is where participants drop out of the study. Often, the participants who leave the study are the most interesting (e.g. they moved abroad, went to prison or died unexpectedly) and their departure can make the cohort **unrepresentative** (p22). The longer the study lasts, the worse sample attrition becomes.

- A **retrospective longitudinal study** identifies a cohort who all share a common outcome (such as ending up in prison or being a victim of crime) but then works backwards in time, identifying factors in their life history that brought them to this point. Sample attrition isn't a problem but **incomplete data** is: there might be no record of the background of some of the participants, especially if they have had unusual lives (moved around a lot, changed their identity, been homeless).

The advantage of longitudinal studies is that they reveal **patterns and trends** over time (p9) which is why they are popular with Positivists. However, they can also explore a person's entire **life course**, which is a concept that Interpretivists think is important.

The disadvantage of longitudinal studies is that they are **expensive** (since the researchers and perhaps the participants need to be paid). If the researchers become too close to the cohort they will lose their **objectivity** (p10). However, these problems are reduced in retrospective studies.

METHODS PROFILE: MESSNER & COOKY* (2021) VS HECHT ET AL* (2020)

Michael Messner & Cheryl Cooky carried out a 30-year **prospective longitudinal study** but the cohort was not a group of people but a selection of TV channels: this is a **content analysis** (p64) where researchers study the content of media documents. Starting in 1989, the researchers recorded 3 two-week segments of sports coverage from 3 Los Angeles TV networks and repeated this procedure every 5 years, bringing in the sports highlights show on ESPN (a digital sports channel) in 2004. Their aim was to find out how women's sports were being presented.

Messner & Cooky are able to chart the proportion of time given to men's and women's sport (95% devoted to men in 2019) and how this changes over time – or rather, how it *hasn't* changed much in 30 years. They identify changes in the style of presentation. For example, in the 1990s TV coverage often sexualised women sports players but in 2019 this switched to **'gender-bland' reporting** which doesn't treat the women as sex objects but does present their sports as boring, with none of the passion and excitement that characterises the way male sports are presented.

Hecht et al (p30) also make use of a longitudinal study carried out by the **Office for National Statistics**. The cohorts are people in the UK born at certain times: the first cohort was people born 1955-61; these people were surveyed in 1971 aged 10-16 and again in 1991 aged 30-36. Hecht compares them to cohorts born 1965-71 (surveyed in 2001) and 1975-81 (surveyed in 2011). The ONS survey records where the cohorts lived and their social class as well as where they were born and their social class at birth.

INTERPRETATION OF DATA

Once data has been collected, sociologists have to make sense of it. There are two main methods: **quantitative methods** and **qualitative methods**.

Qualitative data interpretation makes use of **qualitative data** (descriptions in words, *c.f.* p17) by putting these descriptions into categories; this creates **categorical data**. The process to do this is called coding. Usually, a researcher will go through a written version of the data (a **transcript**) and apply codes to certain phrases, statements, attitudes or behaviours.

Categorical data can be shown as **percentages** and put into **pie charts** or **histograms**. The **mode** is an important measure for categorical data: it shows the most popular category or the most frequently occurring code.

Qualitative data is also interpreted through **semiotics**. Semiotics is the study of signs and symbols, which for a sociologist can mean the language people use, the way they dress and act and the meaning behind body language and gestures. Semiotics is an important technique for Interpretivists, but it has been adopted by many **Neo-Marxists** who use semiotics to show how ordinary language or behaviour is actually a symbolic form of oppression or resistance to Capitalism.

METHODS PROFILE: MESSNER & COOKY* (2021, cont'd)

Messner & Cooky (p37) use **codes** to analyse the qualitative data taken from recorded TV sports programmes. The codes include gender of sport (men's, women's, neutral), type of sport (basketball, football, golf, tennis, etc.) and competitive level of the sport (professional, college, high school, etc.). Codes also include production values such as the use of music, the use of graphics, and the inclusion of interviews and/or game highlights.

The researchers also use **semiotics** to analyse what sports commentators are saying and what TV cameras focus on. They conclude that in the 1990s, TV commentary focused on women sports players' bodies, especially their sexual characteristics. However, they observe that this is less common now, but that women's sports are covered in a 'gender-bland' way that lacks passion and excitement.

Quantitative data interpretation analyses **quantitative data** (p7) and creates **numerical data**. Usually, a researcher performs statistical analyses looking for **patterns and trends**. Important measures for this sport of data are the **mean** and **median** (which are **measures of central tendency**, revealing the data that is 'in the middle') and **standard deviation** (showing how much scores typically vary above or below the mean).

A more complex type of statistical analysis is **regression analysis**. Regression analyses measure relationships between different variables, taking as-yet-unknown factors into account. A regression analysis will show how one variable changes depending on how other factors alter. This is useful for showing things like how poverty or crime alter when unemployment goes up or down, more or less is spent on policing and benefits are increased or decreased.

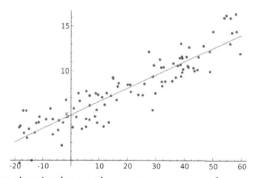

*A **linear regression** showing how a clear pattern emerges from random data points*

┌ ─ ┐

METHODS PROFILE: HECHT ET AL.* (2020, cont'd)

Katharina Hecht's study of social mobility (p30) uses a longitudinal study carried out by the Office for National Statistics. Regression analysis shows whether people are more or less likely to improve their social class (social mobility) in different cohorts when they have similar class backgrounds or levels of education to start with. Hecht also looks at other influencing factors like receiving private education or moving to London. The results show more mobility in the older cohorts (surveyed in 1971) than the younger ones (surveyed in 2001 and 2011).

└ ─ ┘

RELATIONSHIP TO SOCIAL POLICY

Social policy means the laws and programmes created by the Government. They include things like making behaviours illegal (or legalising things that used to be banned) as well as changing benefits and healthcare, altering the curriculum taught in schools and controlling immigration.

Most social policy is intended to solve social problems. **Peter Worsley (1977)** defines a **social problem** is any behaviour that causes *"public friction or private misery."* Crime and poverty are obvious examples but so are domestic violence, school failure, drug abuse and racist discrimination.

Sociology can contribute to social policy in three ways:

1. **Descriptive research:** This is research that aims to describe the nature and scale of a problem, such as how much inequality there is, whether it is growing and who is worst affected by it. **Hecht et al. (2020)** conduct descriptive research by showing that social mobility is less common as elites 'pull away' from the rest of us (p30) – however they do not suggest what should be done about this.
2. **Explanatory research:** This research aims to reveal the causes of social problems – and usually to suggest solutions too. For example, **Wilkinson & Pickett (2009)** conducted explanatory research in their book *The Spirit Level* (p29) by showing that a lot of social problems that are ordinarily thought of as quite separate (such as obesity, violent crime and teenage pregnancies) are in fact related to inequality in society. They suggest that social policies to reduce inequality will reduce these problems too as a 'knock-on effect.'
3. **Evaluative research:** The aim is to research *existing* social policies to see if they are working and make suggestions as to how they can be improved. For example, **Sewell et al. (2021)** produced the **CRED Report** (p27) which found that social policies to reduce ethnic inequality in the UK have been successful, although they make 24 recommendations including changing the way the police deal with minorities and the way ethnic minority children are treated in schools.

Sociological problems are issues that fascinate sociologists but might not be widespread enough to be considered social problems or they might be viewed as not a 'problem' in the normal sense of the word.

Durkheim's fascination with suicide (p12) might be a sociological problem rather than a social problem. Another sociological problem might be **Jones' et al**.'s research into why successful people choose early retirement (p35): taking early retirement isn't a problem (in fact, it sounds rather nice) but it's puzzling for sociologists why some workers choose to do it but others don't.

There is a link to **choice of topic** (p26) because researching social problems often attracts funding, whereas it is much harder to find someone to fund research into sociological problems that don't have a clear link to social policy.

AO2 ILLUSTRATION: WHO FUNDS SOCIAL RESEARCH?

The Office for National Statistics (ONS) funds research into the UK population and publishes data to advise governments on social policy. Since 2008 it has been a **non-ministerial department**, independent of government. This is a huge boost to its credibility as a provider of unbiased data (very important for Positivists) and also a boost for the credibility of Government social policies that are based on ONS-provided data.

Government departments also fund research into areas they manage, such as the **Department of Health & Social Care (DHSC)** or the **Department for Education (DfE)**. This research can have a direct effect on social policy, but these are ministerial departments headed by a politician, so their research is sometimes criticised for being politically biased. The **Commission on Race & Ethnic Disparities (CRED)** was set up in 2020 by the Prime Minister, so the findings of **Sewell et al. (2021,** p27) was seen by critics as politically biased and invalid.

Outside of Government, there are charities and think-tanks that fund research into social problems. The **Centre for Policy Studies** is a Right Wing think tank linked to the New Right. **The Joseph Rowntree Foundation (JRF)** funds research and programmes to reduce poverty in the UK and it claims to be politically neutral. **The Sutton Trust** funds research into improving social mobility. Both were created by millionaire businessmen who were **philanthropists** (people for use their wealth for public good) and this makes some Marxist sociologists question whether they are truly politically neutral.

Research can also be funded by universities – through the **Economic & Social Research Council (ESRC)** – or by media organisations like the **BBC**. These bodies are more likely to fund research into interesting sociological problems that aren't related to social policy.

Positivism vs Interpretivism

Positivism was developed by **Auguste Comte** (p12) with the explicit intention of helping governments arrive at the right social policy. Positivism aims to present policymakers with clear statistics about **social problems** and policy recommendations that are completely unbiased (**value-free**, p10). Because Positivism claims to discover the underlying causes of social behaviour (**social facts**), it focuses on explanatory research that is **macro** in scale.

Interpretivists are sceptical about Positivist claims of value-freedom and discovering social facts. They point out that research can never be unbiased and so-called social facts are really just the unexamined assumptions of researchers imposed onto the data. They tend to focus on **sociological problems** rather than social problems and their independence from government funding leaves them free to conduct **micro-** scale research and engage in **reflexivity** (p16), even if that sometimes gets in the way of clear findings and concrete solutions.

Consensus vs Conflict

Functionalism and the **New Right** are both consensus perspectives and they tend to take a Positivist view of the relationship between research and social policy. **Charles Murray**'s book *Losing Ground* (1984, p12) was very influential on Right Wing governments in the USA and the UK. Murray employed statistical analyses of crime rates, birth rates and unemployment to demonstrate a social fact that lone parents unwittingly contribute to the growth of an unemployed and semi-criminal underclass. Murray recommends cutting benefits and support for lone-parent families to encourage a return to married parents and working fathers. Since then, the New Right has had a big influence on UK social policy.

Marxism and **Feminism** are conflict perspectives that have a more mixed view of Positivism and social policy. Marxists view the Government as part of the **ruling class** and Feminists often view it as a force for **patriarchy**: both are sceptical about whether social policy can make any difference to the social problems they care about (the exploitation of the poor and of women). Some of them argue that, with all its flaws, the Government is still the best institution for solving social problems; this approach lies behind **Wilkinson & Pickett**'s *The Spirit Level* (2009, p29) which encouraged a Left Wing UK Labour Government to focus on inequality.

Other conflict sociologists see their role as being a 'gadfly' (a stinging insect) that criticises the Government and shows the flaws in social policy. These sociologists seek funding from charities and political think tanks that given them more freedom to criticise. **Hecht et al. (2020**, p30) was funded by the **Sutton Trust**, an educational charity which invests £4 million every year in research and programmes to improve social mobility.

Structuralism vs Social Action

Functionalists, the New Right, Marxists and Feminists all tend to be **structuralists**: they view individuals as shaped by the social structures around them rather than having freewill and independence. Structuralists take a keen interest in social policy because they don't view people as individuals or small groups having the power to change things without help from the Government.

Social Action sociologists see individuals and small groups as able to 'rise up' and challenge or change social structures. They often take **Max Weber** (p18) as an inspiration. **Jones et al. (2012)** share **Ulrich Beck**'s view that research participants are **quasi-subjects** (p35) who partly reflect the social structures around them but also partly forge their own path in life.

Social Action tends to adopt **Interpretivist** methods and focus on **micro**-scale research that has little connection to social policy. However, some **Feminists** and **Neo-Marxists** have adopted Social Action theories – especially the ideas of **labelling theory** – and focused on minority groups and subcultures. The research by the **Centre for Contemporary Cultural Studies** into 1970s **Punks** is a good example of this. This research tends to be into **sociological problems** but it can be used to challenge popular stereotypes about (for example) ethnic minorities or youth subcultures.

Strengths & Weaknesses

There are two big incentives for carrying out research that relates to social policy: **(1)** your research will be studied by policymakers and might make a difference to people's lives and **(2)** your research has a better chance of being funded, since there are lots of government bodies, think tanks and charities interested in social policy too.

The main disadvantage to such research is that with funding comes interference – and even if the funder does *not* interfere with your research, there may be a suspicion that your research is biased because of who funded it. Research for ministerial departments or politically-motivated think tanks like the **Centre for Policy Studies** always comes with the suspicion of political bias. Some charities, such as **JRF** or the **Sutton Trust**, claim to be politically neutral and have great credibility, but even they get criticised for political bias sometimes.

Avoiding social policy means researchers can investigate without political interference (or accusations of it), but it also means there is less funding and less of a readership for the findings. The **ESRC** funds a lot of research into sociological problems rather than social problems, simply for the sake of furthering our understanding of society. However, this sort of funding is limited and it still tends to follow 'fashions' in universities – for example, research into inequalities affecting ethnic minorities and LGBTQ groups is popular right now because of the attention drawn to these issues by protest organisations like **Black Lives Matter** or **Stonewall**.

Revision: revisit your notes from **paper 1** on Consensus, Conflict and Social Action to add social policy as an evaluation issue

THE RESEARCH PROCESS: A TOOLKIT

We have covered the research process in general, but some aspects of research need closer analysis and a consideration of strengths and weaknesses.

THE SAMPLING PROCESS

A **sample** means the people who participate in research. Research has a **target population** which is all the people the research is investigating and trying to describe. The target population might be as small as *'the boys in this school's Sixth Form'* or as large as *'all the working-class adults in the UK.'* The sample is a small selection of that larger population.

- A **small and tightly defined target population** is quite easy to sample, but the conclusions from the research often won't generalise to other populations. If your target population is boys in your school Sixth Form, the sample might not tell you much about boys of a similar age in other schools. **Interpretivists** (p13) are usually happy with this sort of population.

- A **large target population** means the research's findings will apply to a lot more people, but it's hard to select a sample from such a population. **Positivists** (p6) usually try to study large populations through sampling but they have to use careful sampling techniques to get a sample that is truly **representative**.

A **sampling frame** is a list of everyone in the target population. Sometimes it's easy to acquire a sampling frame; every school will keep a list of all the students enrolled there. However, sometimes there is no complete or reliable sampling frame; there's no 'master list' of everyone who lives in the UK or everyone in a town who is working-class.

Positivism aims to conduct **macro**-level research on large target populations. A sampling frame helps them to gather a sample that is **representative** (p22) – in other words, it is a miniature version of the target population. This enables Positivist researchers to **generalise** conclusions about the sample back to the target population.

Interpretivism aims to conduct **micro**-level research on small target populations. The sampling frame is less important for this sort of research. Interpretivists hope to gain **insights** into the behaviour and attitudes of people involved – and into their own behaviour and attitudes too if they use **reflexivity** (p16). They are less interested in **generalising** to a wider population to propose patterns or trends.

Terminology: Subjects, Participants, Respondents

Older research often refers to the people taking part as the '**subjects**' of research. This term is unfashionable now. It implies that the people involved are like lab rats or guinea pigs being investigated by superior social scientists. Some Positivists really believed research to be like this in the past, but not so much anymore.

Participants is a better term, since it refers to people actively participating in research rather than being studied from above. **Respondents** is another term which focuses on how people respond to the questions and situations that the researchers study.

The replacing of the Positivist term 'subjects' with the more Interpretivist-friendly terms 'participants' and 'respondents' might indicate a shift in methodology going on in Sociology as a whole.

SAMPLING TECHNIQUE: OPPORTUNITY

Opportunity sampling means using the people who are available in a certain place at a certain time. This group of people is termed 'an opportunity sample.'

Opportunity sampling is the **easiest and quickest** sampling technique. It does creates **unrepresentative samples**. People who are all present at a certain place at a certain time typically share characteristics in common (like working in the same job, studying the same subjects). People who don't share these characteristics are unlikely to be present.

Imagine gathering a sample of students from the student lounge during break – but students who have break time duties or meetings won't be present.

Opportunity sampling is also at risk from **bias**, since the researcher might approach people that seem friendly or helpful and avoid people they find threatening or view as boring.

Positivists avoid this technique, because it is unrepresentative and biased, and they aim to be **value-free** (p10). Interpretivists are less critical of opportunity sampling, since they don't put some much emphasis on representativeness, and they can reflect on issues of bias through **reflexivity** (p16).

SAMPLING TECHNIQUE: PURPOSIVE

Purposive sampling means deliberately selecting particular people because they have the characteristics the research is interested in. A 'purposive sample' might be a group of people who are specially invited to take part in research.

Purposive sampling is different from opportunity sampling because it doesn't just use anyone to hand; instead, the researcher goes out and tracks down **special individuals**.

Imagine tracking down students who took part in a demonstration or sit-in because you want to know what motivated them. You will have in mind exactly the people you want to study and no one else will do.

Positivists rarely use this technique, because you **cannot draw patterns and trends** from unusual individuals. This is a technique usually associated with Interpretivists who want to increase their understanding (**verstehen**, p15) of the **social world** of unusual people.

METHODS PROFILE: WILLIS (1977, cont'd)

Paul Willis' *Learning To Labour* (p21) studies a group of 12 working-class schoolboys ('the Lads'), but how did Willis recruit them? Willis describes how they were selected because they were likely to leave school as soon as was legal (aged 16 in the 1970s) and were part of **an anti-school subculture**. Presumably, Willis shared with the teachers the sort of students he was interested in researching and they suggested 'the Lads' as matching this description (*cf.* **gatekeeping**, p49).

Notice how this **purposive sampling** gets round the problem that 'the Lads' would never *choose* to get involved in research. The boys were unusually rebellious even for a tough working-class school: they are the special individuals that purposive sampling can locate and recruit.

SAMPLING TECHNIQUE: SNOWBALL

Snowball sampling is when the researcher makes contact with one person (or a few people) and asks them to recruit other individuals who would be suitable. It is a special sort of **purposive sampling** because the respondents go out and recruit each other rather than all being invited by the researcher. The sample size grows like a snowball as each new recruit recruits more people.

Imagine tracking down a few students who took part in a demonstration and asking them to invite other students whom they know helped organise things behind-the-scenes – as the researcher, you wouldn't know about these other people's involvement.

Snowball sampling is particularly useful when there is **no sampling frame** – particularly if the target population is doing something criminal or which attracts social stigma, so they are unlikely to respond to **volunteer sampling** but they might get involved if someone they trust invites them. Because the respondents recruit more respondents, snowball samples often contain people the researchers would never make contact with by any other method.

As with purposive sampling, which it resembles, this is popular with Interpretivists who want to **understand behaviour on a micro-level**. It is not used much by Positivists, because if you do not recruit your own sample, you **cannot know whether it is representative** of your population.

METHODS PROFILE: HECHT ET AL.* (2020, cont'd)

Katharina Hecht's study of social mobility (p30) mixes Positivist and Interpretivist approaches. She gathered a sample of 30 'elite earners' some of whom were multi-millionaires. Hecht discovered their names in the *Sunday Times Rich List* or because they were well-known figures in the London financial industry. Some of them went on to invite other elite earners that they knew to join in – so this is **snowball sampling technique**.

The response rate was 40%. Hecht reflects that her own class background and her education at the London School of Economics (a prestigious university) made the initial respondents more likely to agree to help: this is an issue of **access** to a hidden group (p49).

SAMPLING TECHNIQUE: VOLUNTEER

Volunteer sampling is when the researcher **advertises the research** and waits for people to volunteer themselves to take part; it is also called **self-selecting sampling** and the group that is recruited this way is a **volunteer sample**.

Volunteer sampling is similar to **purposive sampling** because the researcher can advertise for a particular type of person (or advertise in places or media that this type of person uses). However, it is different because the researcher cannot control exactly who is recruited.

The sample will be biased, but not because of the researcher's biases but rather because of the biases in the participants themselves. Some people are more likely to volunteer (e.g. people interested in Sociology, people with free time, people who need money if the volunteers are being paid) but volunteers are less likely if the research looks embarrassing, boring or dangerous.

Imagine recruiting students who took part in a demonstration by putting up a poster in the student lounge asking everyone who took part in throwing eggs at the Principal's car to come to room 13 at lunch – why would actual demonstrators not turn up?

A common approach is to send the invitation out in the mail or through email. Sending mass surveys through the post is volunteer sampling because anyone who returns a completed survey is volunteering to take part.

Volunteer sampling is useful when there is **no sampling frame** but it is more popular with Positivists than **purposive** or **snowball sampling**, because you can recruit large samples this way from big target populations.

SAMPLING TECHNIQUE: RANDOM

Random sampling is a technique to **remove all bias** from the selection of participants. A group selected in an unbiased way will be a random sample.

*IMPORTANT: 'random' in popular language means 'unplanned' or 'surprising' (as in, you watched a random YouTube video or talked to a random person at a party). THAT IS NOT WHAT IT MEANS IN SOCIOLOGY. **Random means 'selected without bias'** – your YouTube video was not really selected randomly (YouTube's algorithm put it in front of you based on things you had previously watched) nor was the person you talked to at the party truly random (you **chose** to talk to them and there were other people you chose not to talk to). Walking into the student lounge and picking the first dozen people you see is not random sampling – it is opportunity sampling.*

To remove all bias, a **randomisation technique** is needed. This could be the classic **'names from the hat'**: write everyone's name on a separate piece of paper, put all the names in a box or bag, draw out a number of pieces of paper until you reach the sample size you want then recruit those people. Computers apps also produce a randomised sample from a list of names.

The important thing to understand is that it is essential to have a **complete sampling frame** in order to create a random sample.

Creating a random sample of boys from the school Sixth Form is easy because there is a complete sampling frame – the school register. Creating a random sample of teenage boys in a city is not possible because there's no up-to-date master list kept anywhere.

The main problem with randomised sampling is that it **doesn't necessarily create a representative sample**. For example, drawing names from a hat could produce a sample made entirely of boys from one ethnic group. This problem is more likely to occur with small sampling frames. Positivists only use random sampling when they have access to very large sampling frames (like the **UK Census**, *see below*).

Random sampling can also include **inappropriate respondents** who are difficult to track down, who don't want to be in the research or who are unsuitable for studying (perhaps because they don't speak English or have health problems). Interpretivists usually want respondents who will engage with their micro-level research, so they tend to avoid random sampling.

METHODS PROFILE: HECHT ET AL.* (2020, cont'd)

Katharina Hecht's study of social mobility (p30) mixes Positivist and Interpretivist approaches. Hecht uses the **ONS Longitudinal Study** to get data on social mobility in different decades. The **Office for National Statistics** (p40) uses the **UK Census** as its sampling frame. The Census is a survey carried out every 10 years to gather data on every household in the country (*c.f.* p57). The ONS then takes a random sample of 1% of the sampling frame: about 500,000 people in each cohort. The sheer size makes it likely that the sample is **representative**.

The Census doesn't include *everybody* in the country – you won't appear on the Census if you are homeless or an illegal immigrant. However, Hecht was only interested in data from the ONS Longitudinal Study about people moving into the 'elite earners' group and most of these people will be on the Census (they have homes and they are not in the country illegally).

STRATIFIED SAMPLING

This is an improvement on **random sampling** and makes use of randomisation but it also makes sure the sample contains the right amounts of the right sort of people.

Stratified sampling involves dividing your target population into groups (or 'strata') and making sure your sample has the same strata in the same proportions. Once the strata have been decided upon, they are filled by random allocation, just like random sampling.

Creating a stratified sample of boys from a school Sixth Form involves identifying the strata in the target population – such as 60% in Year 12 and 40% in Year 13, perhaps 30% doing Science courses – then using school registers to randomly select students for each strata.

47

Stratified sampling requires a **complete sampling frame** and also a lot of **information about the target population** and that information might not be available – for example, you might want a strata of students from particular class backgrounds but the school wouldn't keep data like that on record.

Stratified sampling is the 'holy grail' of Positivist research because as well as being **unbiased** it creates **highly representative samples**.

However, Interpretivists argue that the strata themselves conceal **researcher imposition** (p16). This is because the choice of what strata include or leave out reflects researcher bias; for example, a researcher might not bother to include 'religion' as a strata but assuming that religion isn't relevant to social behaviour is a biased assumption. Since there are an infinite number of strata, researchers can never know if they are ignoring important strata or not (should you have a strata for handedness? how about star signs?) and trying to include every strata you can think of 'just in case' would make the research time consuming and over-complicated.

SAMPLING TECHNIQUE: SYSTEMATIC

Systematic sampling is a variation on **random sampling**. Instead of randomising the sampling frame, the researcher goes through the sampling frame selecting every n^{th} person from the list (e.g. every 5th or 10th or 100th person). This produces a systematic sample.

Systematic sampling has the same strengths and weaknesses as **random sampling**. In particular, it requires a **complete sampling frame**. Counting out every n^{th} person guarantees that the sample will be more spread out, whereas a randomly selected sample could draw from people who are 'clumped together.' This makes a systematic sample more representative than a purely random one if the sampling frame is arranged in a particular order (say, ordering people by age would produce a systematic sample of all ages).

SAMPLING TECHNIQUE: QUOTA

Quota sampling is an alternative to **random sampling** and an improvement on **purposive sampling**.

A quota sample is recruited by filling strata that match the target population, just like a **stratified sample** (*see above*). However, you do not fill each strata randomly. Instead, you fill each strata using a non-random method, like **opportunity**, **purposive** or **volunteer sampling**.

Quota sampling is useful when you want your sample to be **representative,** but you **do not have a complete sampling frame**. Because the respondents are either volunteering themselves or being chosen specially by the researcher, some **bias** is inevitable.

Quota sampling is often used by companies trying to gauge public opinion – for example, approaching people in the street with clipboards to carry out surveys, but making sure to get data from a certain number of men, women, minorities, age groups, etc.

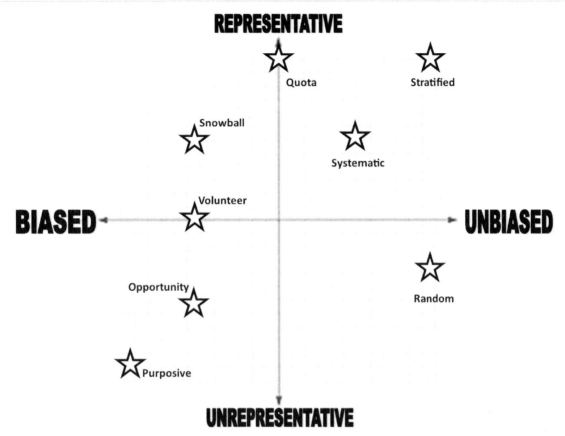

This chart might help you visualise the way different sampling techniques relate. **Positivists** aim to use unbiased procedures to gather highly representative samples (top right quadrant); **Interpretivists** are comfortable with biased procedures so long as they are reflexively addressed and they often don't care about generalising conclusions from a representative sample.

ACCESS & GATEKEEPING

Access means the ability to make contact with potential respondents and recruit them into a sample. There are several problems with access faced by sociologists:

- **Protected groups:** Some groups are protected from researchers, often because of safeguarding issues. For example, children, the mentally ill, victims of abuse and people inside 'closed institutions' like prisons or women's refuges. In order to get access to these groups, a **gatekeeper** (e.g. a parent, head teacher, doctor or prison governor) has to allow it.

- **Hidden groups:** These groups are hard to locate and make contact with; some live 'off the grid' or have a language barrier, others deliberately avoid contact with the authorities (e.g. deviants). A **gatekeeper** is often needed to put the researcher in touch (e.g. a community leader, translator or gang member). Wealthy people can also be hard to gain access to (*c.f.* Hecht et al., p45)

- **Hostile groups:** These groups are easy to find but they don't want to take part in research; this often includes subcultures who are suspicious of outsiders as well as criminal gangs or religious sects. **Gatekeepers** might be members who can vouch for the researcher and make introductions.

Snowball sampling (p45) is particularly useful for gaining access to hidden or hostile groups once initial contact has been made. **Volunteer sampling** (p46) is particularly ineffective with these groups (it's not obvious how to advertise to hidden groups and hostile groups don't want to volunteer).

Gatekeeping means managing access to groups. With protected groups, the gatekeeper is someone in authority whose permission is needed to recruit respondents. The gatekeeper will be concerned about the rights and wellbeing of respondents and won't want them to get involved in research that might be stressful or expose them to stigma, abuse or stereotyping.

With hidden or hostile groups, the gatekeeper is someone who can put the researcher in touch with respondents, perhaps by translating or vouching for the researcher's good intentions. This sort of gatekeeper is a 'friend on the inside.'

Gatekeepers often have access to a **sampling frame** (a list of all the members of the group).

METHODS PROFILE: GENTLEMAN* (2009)

Amelia Gentleman is a journalist who spent 4 days observing 26 elderly residents in a care home (Monmouth Court in Ipswich, p50). She carried out **overt observations** (p60) and **unstructured interviews** (p58) with residents and staff and published her findings in *The Guardian*.

The care home is a closed institution, and the elderly residents are a protected group: some are ill, confused or depressed and not in a position to **consent** (p51) to participate in research; there is a danger a journalist could misrepresent the care home as an evil place, make the residents look foolish or a burden on others or make the staff look uncaring.

The Matron is the **gatekeeper** and she allows Gentleman to visit the public areas of the care home (the day lounge) and interview selected residents and staff. This makes the sample a **purposive sample** (p44) carried out in negotiation with the gatekeeper.

ETHICS

The **British Sociological Society (BSA)** lays out a set of ethical guidelines for researchers to follow. Breaking these guidelines can create distrust, which lowers the **validity** of research (p19) as well as making it harder for future researchers to gain **access** to respondents (p49). Sociologists need to be in good standing with the BSA to work in universities and get their research published, so breaking the ethical guidelines can ruin a sociologist's career.

There are six ethical guidelines:

1. **Consent:** Respondents should be aware that they are involved in a research project and its purpose; they should give **informed consent** to taking part.

   - Some respondents cannot give informed consent: children are considered too young and people with mental health problems are not competent to do this. A parent or carer could consent on their behalf.

   - Some groups have to be studied without their consent, because they wouldn't be doing what they are doing if they knew they were being studied (e.g. criminals) or else would not respond truthfully to questions.

2. **Deception:** Researchers should not lie to respondents about the purpose of the research or their own identity. They should not feign friendship in order to gain data.

   - Sometimes deception is unavoidable if the researcher has to keep their identity secret (e.g. **covert observations**, p60). The data gained from 'going undercover' can be so valuable (e.g. to **social policy**, p39) that it justifies deception.

3. **Confidentiality:** Research should not be intrusive. Respondents should have their true names and backgrounds concealed – many researchers use pseudonyms (fake names) for respondents. Promising **confidentiality** can increase trust, leading to respondents giving more **valid** data.

   - Confidentiality includes not revealing locations or institutions that might identify the respondents.

   - Confidentiality can come into conflict with **integrity** (*below*) if the respondents do or reveal something illegal or immoral.

4. **Protection:** Respondents should be protected from harm. This includes not being asked distressing questions or being put in stressful situations. It also includes not being exposed to ridicule or punishment (such as losing your job) when the research is published. **Respondent validation** (p34) is an opportunity to make sure that everyone agrees with what is being published.

   - Not everyone agrees on the definition of 'harm.' For example, asking questions about experiences of abuse or crime can trigger anxiety. Gaining **informed consent** (*above*) is important for justifying this.

5. **Integrity:** Researchers should not carry out illegal or immoral acts while pursuing research. If they come into possession of 'guilty knowledge' (e.g. a respondent confesses to a crime) then they should report it to the police or other authorities.

- This can come into conflict with **privacy** when the researcher promises to keep identities confidential and **protection** when researchers suffer sanctions (get arrested, relationships end, fired from their job) because of what was revealed during the research.

6. **Safety:** Researchers should not put themselves or their research assistants in danger.

- Some research is unavoidably risky, such as observing criminals. Other research can create anxiety, such as studying people who are dying or listening to testimonies of abuse. This links to **choice of topic** (p26) because the risks of some topics have to be justified by the benefits to be gained (e.g. informing **social policy**).

> **Research:** visit the British Sociological Society website (https://www.britsoc.co.uk/ethics) and read the ethical guidelines yourself – notice the extra guidelines on digital research that will be important for **3A: Globalisation & the Digital Social World**.

METHODS PROFILE: WILLIS (1977) vs GENTLEMAN* (2009)

Paul Willis (c.f. p21) observes 12 schoolboys in lessons and with their teachers, parents and later their employers. He gains **consent** from their teachers and (we assume) their parents to do this; later, he gains consent from the boys themselves once they turned 16. There was no deception and Willis keeps their identities **confidential**, referring to their school by the fictional name of Hammertown Boys School. There are no issues with protection or safety, but Willis' **integrity** could be questioned: he witnessed 'the Lads' carrying out acts of vandalism (setting off fire extinguishers), bullying and racist abuse, but did not intervene or report anything. Of course, if he *had* intervened, he would have lost the trust of the boys.

Amelia Gentleman (c.f. p50) observes 26 elderly residents in a care home over 4 days. Most of the residents are depressed and some suffer from dementia; several are dying: Gentleman needs **consent** from the Matron (and probably family members) on behalf of the residents. Gentleman's article states '*Names of residents have been changed and some details have been altered to obscure identities*' – this ensures **confidentiality** and **protection**. There is no problem with **deception** and **integrity** but **safety** is an issue: Gentleman reports residents who are dying and carers with tragic financial problems; she finds the atmosphere "*dispiriting*" and the research must have taken an emotional toll on her.

NB. Amelia Gentleman is a journalist, not a sociologist, and doesn't need to be a member of the BSA or follow its guidelines. However, there is a similar journalistic code of ethics.

EXAM PRACTICE: THEORY & METHODS

The OCR exam has four questions in **Paper 2 Section A**, based on two source items:

Source A

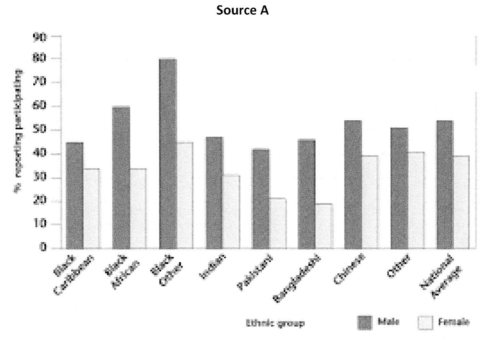

Source: Sport England's Sports Participation & Ethnicity in England – National Survey 1999/2000

Source B

Dr William Tantam spent more than a year in Jamaica studying amateur football or 'pick-up ball' in a rural community. For 14 months he played football every weekday with the same group of players. He socialised with them and conducted interviews to discover what role football played in their lives. 'Pick-up ball' could be dangerous, since it is played in the street with cars passing.

One team was of younger (20s-30s), poorer men; the other of older (40s-50s), wealthier men. Most had participated in an annual inter-school tournament. Those from poorer backgrounds had 'skipped class' to concentrate on football, hoping to win scholarships – after gaining poor qualifications, they had taken up low-paid and precarious jobs. Those from wealthier backgrounds had been discouraged from participating in schoolboy football – later they migrated to get a better education then returned to Jamaica for well-paid jobs as doctors or teachers.

The rural community was divided along lines of wealth and class, but football offered a way for the men to interact as equals. The younger players were less interested in winning a match; more interested in demonstrating creative or skilful moves. Due to the pressure of 'playing for a scholarship,' they had developed an individualistic form of football . The older group focused on team play and winning matches. While the two teams shared a field, they were playing two very different games with different aims.

1. Summarise the data shown in **Source A**. [4 marks: 4 AO2]

*Make **two** points about the data. It is vital that you quote actual figures from the graph and draw conclusions from them (or you are not 'summarising' the data, only restating it). For example, only 20% of Bangladeshi women report participating in sport. In order to summarise, you need to say whether this is higher or lower than Bangladeshi males or women from other groups.*

2. With reference to **Source B**, explain **two** reasons why sociologists might have problems with access to research participants. [6 marks: 2 AO1 + 4 AO2]

Write a couple of sentences about each reason. You might focus on hostility, access to wealthy groups or gatekeepers. You need to support each reason with an example from the source – a really good idea is to quote something from the source.

3. With reference to **Source A**, explain **one** advantage and **one** disadvantage of sociologists gathering primary data. [10 marks: 4 AO2 + 6 AO3]

Write two short paragraphs, one about an advantage (such as revealing social facts, operationalising your own concepts, relationship to social policy) and one about a disadvantage (such as problems with access and gatekeeping, time and expense, sampling problems, ethical problems). You need to support each reason with an example from the source – a really good idea is to quote a number (or approximate number) from the graph.

4. Using **Source B** and your wider sociological knowledge, explain and evaluate ethical issues in researching differences between classes. [25 marks: 5 AO1 + 5 AO2 + 15 AO3]

*Write four paragraphs/arguments – two ethical strengths and two ethical weaknesses would work well. Each paragraph should introduce a sociological idea with an example or comparison from **Source B**. Each paragraph should finish off with a developed evaluation (see **Chapter 4** for this). For example, you could write about the importance of establishing trust through consent, honesty and confidentiality, but the problems of misrepresenting poorer people as failures or losers or the safety issues of street sports.*

In questions 2-3 you can pick up the AO1 marks from using sociological terminology and relating things to sociological debates (e.g. Positivism vs Interpretivism). Named sociologists and studies aren't particularly important.

Question 4 is a full essay in which you are invited to deploy *"your wider sociological knowledge"* so famous sociologists definitely belong in your answer and a comparison to **Willis'** study would help (he looks at class differences between schoolboys) as would **Hecht et al.** (Hecht used her university background to get access to a wealthy group).

CHAPTER THREE – RESEARCH METHODS

Now that you are familiar with the theoretical basis of the research process, it's time to look at research methods themselves.

Structured/Controlled Methods

These methods involve planning everything beforehand. Questionnaires will have closed questions, interviews will be entirely scripted, observations will take place in artificial environments that the researcher has set up and use pre-written checklists.

The advantage of doing this is that it gives the researcher control over what happens. This is important for **Positivists**, who want to be as **scientific** as possible (p6). It helps the researcher study a **sampling frame** and recruit a **randomised sample** from it (p46). In particular, it enables the research to **operationalise** what they are studying (p31) in a way that can be measured or counted – and that leads to the **interpretation of quantitative data** (p37).

The disadvantage of this sort of preparation and control is that the research can become rigid, superficial and unrealistic: questions don't probe deeply, interviews become stilted and one-sided, observations become artificial. It's difficult to **generalise** (p22) the findings of such research to real life, where behaviour is messier, more unpredictable and more varied. Interpretivists complain that this sort of research doesn't reveal much about the **meaning of the social world** (p14).

Unstructured/Naturalistic Methods

These methods involve not planning everything beforehand, in favour or more realism, authenticity and spontaneity. Questionnaires will have open questions that can be answered in ways the researcher doesn't predict, interviews will be unscripted, observations will take place in real-life settings and abandon checklists in favour of trying to share what ordinary people are experiencing.

It's important to appreciate that this sort of research isn't careless, 'anything goes' or fly-by-the-seat-of-your-pants. A lot of preparation has to go into it. Imagine interviewing someone without pre-written questions: you would have to give a lot of thought to what this person is like, what they might say, how you might react.

The advantage of doing this is that it helps the researcher understand (***verstehen*** – p15) the social world. It leads to the **interpretation of qualitative data** (p37) which is much more meaningful. This is important for **Interpretivists**, who value a **subjective but personal understanding** of social behaviour. Moreover, the research is authentic and can be **generalised** (p22) to real life.

The disadvantage is the lack of **scientific objectivity** (p10). In particular, the research lacks **reliability** (p20). Qualitative data is more likely to show **bias**, it doesn't reveal **patterns and trends** (p9) and it is less easy to analyse in a way that can help inform **social policy** (p39).

RESEARCH METHODS: A TOOLKIT

There are three main methods for gathering empirical data: **questionnaires**, **interviews** and **observations**. 'Empirical' means based on first-hand experience and the evidence of the five senses. **Ethnography**, **content analyses** and **statistical data** are best understood as variations of these methods. For example, content analyses are really a type of observation focused on a media document while statistical data is often taken from large-scale surveys involving questionnaires.

METHOD: QUESTIONNAIRES

Questionnaires are also known as **surveys** or **self-reports**. A questionnaire is a set of written questions and the respondent has to write their answers.

- **Closed questions** are questions that force the respondent to choose from a set of possible answers. The simplest closed question is the yes/no question; other examples include multiple-choice questions and checklists. These questions produce **quantitative data** (you can count the number of people who choose each answer or assign a different score to each answer) which can be turned into **statistical data** (p37).

- **Open questions** are questions that allow respondents to answer in any way they like. The simplest open question is *'Explain in your own words ...'* This allows respondents to offer their own unique viewpoint, but it produces **qualitative data**. There is also the risk of answers being unclear or illegible and of better-educated respondents writing in more detail than less-educated ones.

The main advantages of questionnaires is they can be distributed to very **large samples** (through the mail, online, etc) and **do not require trained research assistants** to administer them.

There are many disadvantages to questionnaires. They require the respondent to be able to read and often read to quite a high standard – lengthy questionnaires with technical language can be very off-putting. They might have to be translated into other languages.

Writing a clear, concise questionnaire is not easy to do. Questions can be muddled or interpreted in ways the researcher didn't intend. Another problem is **leading questions**: questions which are worded in a way that encourages a particular answer. A related problem is **affirmation bias**, which is the tendency for respondents to answer *'Yes'* to any question rather than think deeply about it. However, a **pilot study** (p32) could identify these problems in advance.

A lot of people **don't like filling out questionnaires** unless they are being rewarded in some way which is way a lot of consumer surveys come with a free pen or offer to include the respondent in a prize draw. However, because **people are unsupervised while they complete questionnaires** you cannot know if they are taking it seriously or even *who* precisely is answering the questions.

AO2 ILLUSTRATION: NATIONAL SURVEYS IN THE UK

The biggest national survey in the UK is the **Census** which happens every 10 years (recently in 2021, or 2022 in Scotland). The Census provides the UK Government with data about the **demographics** (population make-up) of the UK. The results are published by the **Office for National Statistics** (**ONS**, p40) and are used by sociologists.

Every household has to return a Census form (by post or online) and there is a £1000 fine for failing to do so or returning false information about the people in your household. People who don't have a household (e.g. the homeless) might not appear in the Census. Only one question in the Census is optional and this is the question asking '*What is your religion?*'

Based on 2001 data, about 94% of people complete the Census and data on the rest is either gathered in follow up surveys or statistically calculated from tends. The final results are considered to represent 100% of the UK population.

Other national surveys include the **British Social Attitudes Survey** (3000 respondents every year to gather data on changing norms and values), the **Crime Survey for England & Wales** (CSEW, asks 50,000 respondents about the experience of crime in the previous 12 months) and the **Labour Force Survey** (gathers data about employment from 44,000 households every quarter).

Research: Find out more about these surveys and visit the YouGov.co.uk site (despite its name, not a government-run organisation)

METHODS PROFILE: MARTIN & BLINDER* (2020)

Nicole Martin & Scott Blinder published *Biases At The Ballot Box* **(2020)** which was an investigation into the way political candidates are supported or penalised based on their ethnicity.

The researchers emailed a web-based questionnaire to members of the public who had been part of an online **YouGov survey** into voting intentions in the 2017 UK General Election. This was a **quota sample** (p48) of 7903 respondents that was quite representative of British voters.

The questionnaire provided a profile of two (fictional) political candidates, including their views on immigration and law & order: the candidates were either White, Black Caribbean or Pakistani. The question was: '*Which of these candidates would you rather have as your MP?*' which is a **closed question**.

The researchers used this quantitative data to assess the popularity of political candidates based on their ethnicity of the candidate, the candidate's policies and the ethnicity and gender of the respondents. They found that Pakistani candidates were less popular than White ones offering the same policies, which can be **generalised** to show racist biases in UK voting.

METHOD: INTERVIEWS

Interviews are like questionnaires but are conducted face-to-face (or over the telephone or Internet). The interviewer asks the questions and the interviewee answers them.

- **Structured interviews** are essentially questionnaires that are read aloud, with all the questions scripted in advance. This is much slower than a questionnaire and more expensive, but the interviewer doesn't have to be particularly well trained and might be able to explain questions the interviewee doesn't understand. Because the questions are always the same, they are **reliable** (p20).

- **Unstructured interviews** do not have pre-scripted questions. They resemble a normal conversation, with questions arising out of the previous answer. This is good for establish trust, **empathy and rapport** (p15). It's ideal for sensitive topics, because questions can be phrased differently to avoid distressing the interviewee (which is important for **ethics**, p51). However, the interviewer must be well-trained, and this method is **unreliable**, since every interview will turn out very differently.

- **Semi-structured interviews** combine the two previous approaches: the interview proceeds like a conversation but there are pre-scripted questions that must be asked. This produces an interview which is **quite reliable** and allows the interviewer to ask follow-up questions and pursue topics that the interviewee brings up. As with unstructured interviews, the interviewer must be well-trained.

Interviews don't require the respondent to be able to read – although the interviewer and interviewee must share a language so translators might be needed. **Trained research assistants** are needed for interviews, although the training needed to administer a structured interview is pretty basic.

Interviews have the same problems with leading questions as questionnaires. There is an additional problem of **investigator effects**: this is when the interviewer influences the answers through their tone, facial expression or body language (probably without realising it). Training interviewers not to do this is quite difficult, but **pilot studies** (p32) help identify the problem.

A related problem is when the researcher has **social characteristics** that might influence the interviewee, such as being a different race, gender, age or social class.

The main disadvantage of interviews is that they are **time-consuming**, which means they can't be used with large samples the way that questionnaires can.

The main advantages are the **detailed qualitative data** they gather and the **naturalistic and authentic** way they do this. An unstructured interview can be so naturalistic that the interviewee doesn't even realise they are being interviewed (though there are **ethical issues of deception** with this, p51). The scripted questions in a structured or semi-structured interview can be **closed questions** (p56), which means that interviews can gather quantitative data too.

METHODS PROFILE: HECHT ET AL.* (2020) vs GENTLEMAN* (2009)

Katharina Hecht's study of social mobility (p30) includes interviews with 30 elite earners. Hecht conducts **semi-structured interviews**. She encourages the interviewees to discuss their attitudes to their jobs, money and fairness in society. Hecht also asks pre-planned questions about whether they consider themselves to be high-earners, whether the view inequality as fair and whether they regard their wealth as a reward for their talent or hard work.

Amelia Gentleman's research into care homes for the elderly (p50) includes interviews with the residents and the staff. These are **unstructured interviews**, because Gentleman wants the respondents to offer their own views based on their own experiences: Violet describes having to sell her flat to pay the bills at the care home, Miranda wants to talk about her childhood in the 1930s. The staff offer their perspectives: an Iraqi student nurse is surprised that the British abandon their elderly relatives in care homes and is dismayed how rarely those relatives visit. A set of pre-written questions would not have produced these spontaneous responses.

METHOD: OBSERVATIONS

Observations are different from questionnaires and interviews, because instead of respondents telling you about their experiences, relationships or attitudes, you observe their behaviour and from this you can draw conclusions about their experiences, relationships or attitudes.

In some ways, observing behaviour is ***better*** than respondents telling you about things: respondents might exaggerate or conceal the truth or else they might not know what's going on.

In other ways, observing behaviour is ***worse*** than respondents telling you about things, because your interpretation of their behaviour might not be accurate (**valid**) and this is particularly likely if the people you are observing are from a different class, culture or subculture.

- **Controlled vs naturalistic observations:** Controlled observations are more common in Psychology than Sociology, because they take place in artificial conditions. Naturalistic observations are more common in Sociology and take place is a **real-life situation**, with the participants going about their ordinary business (e.g. employees in a workplace, students in a classroom, shoppers in a mall).

- **Structured vs unstructured observations:** Structured observations have a pre-prepared **checklist** (or **observational schedule**) and only behaviour on the checklist is recorded; this can be tallied later to produce **quantitative data** (p37). Unstructured observations use a blank notepad or recording device and the researcher records **qualitative data** as the situation unfolds. With unstructured observations there's a greater risk of missing things or focusing on the wrong things, but the researcher is free to focus on interesting developments even if they didn't plan for them to happen.

- **Participant vs direct observations:** In a participant observation the researcher joins in the activity with the people being observed, but in a direct observation the researcher stands back and concentrates on observing. It's easier to pay attention during direct observation but participant observation might produce more insight into the people being observed, making it less likely you will misinterpret their behaviour (greater **validity**).

- **Overt vs covert observations:** Overt observations are obvious and announced: the researcher is clearly visible and it's known that she is observing behaviour. Covert observations are secret: the researcher is hidden from view or appears to be just another member of the public. People are more likely to change their behaviour if they know they are being observed (**reducing validity**) but there are **ethical issues** (**consent** and **deception**) with covert observations and sometimes practical problems too (how can you hide the fact that you are making notes on what people do?).

Observations have greater **validity** than questionnaires/interviews, because you are seeing what people actually do in a situation, rather than recording their attitudes or intentions. Electoral polls show that there is a big difference between the way people ***say*** they are going to vote in surveys and the way they ***actually*** vote on the day of the election.

On the other hand, there is a problem of **misinterpretation** with observations. **Interpretivists** argue that the solution is for the observer to embed himself in the culture or community of the people he is observing and understand it 'from the inside' (*c.f.* **ethnography**, p61).

Observations are **time consuming** and require **trained researchers**, especially the sort of 'embedded' observations recommended by Interpretivists. Observations are limited to quite **small samples** and, except for controlled observations that sociologists rarely use, **it isn't possible to randomise** the samples either. This leads to criticism (especially from Positivists) that the samples are **unrepresentative and biased**.

METHODS PROFILE: GENTLEMAN* (2009, cont'd)

Amelia Gentleman's research into life in a care home for the elderly (p50) was a **naturalistic observation**, because it took place in a real care home with real residents and staff going about their day-to-day business.

It was also an **unstructured observation**: the researcher went in with an open mind rather than a checklist of things she expected to see.

It was a **direct observation**: Gentleman did not join the staff in washing and feeding residents and cleaning their rooms; she did not join in the conversations and card games of the residents. She stood back and recorded what she saw and heard.

It was an **overt observation**. Everyone knew that Gentleman was a journalist from *The Guardian* who was writing an article on them. The staff might have pretended to be busier than usual and the residents might have been tense and self-conscious. Gentleman noticed how *"dispiriting"* the *"joyless inertia"* of the day room was with no one speaking to each other – she attributes this to the culture of the care home, but it might just be a reaction to the presence of an outsider. This lowers the **validity** of her conclusions.

On the other hand, Gentleman visited the care home over 4 days, which is time for people to get used to her presence.

METHOD: ETHNOGRAPHY

Ethnography means writing about culture, but it specifically refers to a distinctive **Interpretivist** methodology. Ethnography is not a separate way of gathering data from the ones previously described; instead, it means carrying out **interviews** and **observations** in a certain sort of way.

The original ethnography involved researchers going to live with unusual communities for long periods of time, until they developed a deep understanding of the culture 'from the inside' and understood its norms and values like a native member. **Margaret Mead**'s 1935 fieldwork among the tribes of New Guinea that you learned about in **1A: Socialisation, Culture & Identity** is this sort of ethnography. Mead lived with the Arapesh, Mundugumor and Tchambuli tribes, learned some of their language and took part in the festivals and meetings. She used the insights to reflect on sex and sexuality in her own American culture afterwards.

Ethnographers today don't have to live with isolated tribes on remote islands. Ethnography now means **a systematic attempt to participate in a group, community or subculture in order to understand it**:

- **Participant observations:** it's important for ethnographers to take part in the culture they are studying and be a member of the community, not an outsider looking in

- **Unstructured interviews:** ethnographers use naturalistic methods and want to engage with the people they are studying in the way that these people treat each other, such as normal conversation

- **No questionnaires:** surveys remind everyone that the researcher is an 'expert' seeking information and the respondents are providing her with data; ethnography usually avoids this artificial and divisive approach

- **Longitudinal design** (p36): Ethnography is not about taking a 'snapshot' of a community, but rather experiencing how the community reacts to changes over time; most ethnographic research will last for weeks or even years.

- **Reflexivity** (p16): Ethnographers should reflect on how their presence in a community might affect it as well as how joining a community affects them and teaches them to view their own culture in a new light

Is **Gentleman (2009**, p50**)** an ethnographic study? Gentleman visits the care home over 4 days and carries out naturalistic observations and interviews. However, she doesn't participate in the community she is studying: she doesn't get a job there working undercover as a nurse or disguise herself as an elderly resident. She isn't really there long enough to get 'inside' the culture of either the staff or the residents. So, there are ethnographic *aspects* to Gentleman's research, but it falls short of being 'proper' ethnography.

You can evaluate ethnography by writing about the strengths and weaknesses of **participant observations** (p60) and **unstructured interviews** (p58) and **qualitative interpretations** (p37).

Ethnography has strengths of its own. The idea of getting 'inside' a culture and experiencing the social world the way the natives do is very appealing for **Interpretivists**: it focuses on **understanding (*verstehen*, p15)** and **empathy and rapport**. It can be very useful for dispelling myths about other cultures or subcultures and this can have implications for **social policy** (p39).

However, ethnography **takes a long time** (and expense) and demands a lot of **commitment and training** for researchers (who might need to learn another language). Joining a community 'in disguise' has **ethical implications (consent** and **deception**, p51) and this causes problems if the researcher forms friendships with the people being studied without telling them who she really is. Ethnographers prefer **overt observations**, hoping that the sheer amount of time they spend with the community will make them familiar and accepted, but some groups cannot be studied overtly (e.g. criminal gangs).

A final criticism is that **the sort of understanding ethnographers seek might actually be impossible**. It might be that no amount of time spent in another culture ever really gives you the outlook of someone who grew up in it. Researchers risk imposing their own ideas and beliefs onto the group they are studying. For example, **Derek Freeman (1983)** accuses Mead of describing norms and values in the tribes she lived with that didn't really exist. Mead very much *wanted* to find different gender roles and sexual attitudes in these non-Western cultures and convinced herself that she had.

ETHNOGRAPHY VS ETHNOMETHODOLOGY

Ethnography is in the OCR Specification, and it is described above. **Ethnomethodology** sounds similar but it isn't in the Specification and won't feature in the Exam. Ethnomethodology is focusing on how people make sense of their social world.

METHODS PROFILE: MOORE & CONN* (1985)

Patricia Moore & Charles Conn wrote *Disguised: A True Story* **(1985)** about 27-year-old Moore's experiences of going through life disguised as a 85-year-old woman ('Old Pat').

Moore carried out a **covert unstructured participant observation**; she put on makeup to make her look wrinkly, wore glasses that blurred her vision, wrapped bandages around her body so she was hunched over, plugged her ears so she couldn't hear well, and wore uneven shoes so she was forced to walk with a stick.

Over a 3-year period between 1979-82, Moore played 'Old Pat' in 114 US cities in 14 States, as well as 2 Canadian Provinces. She was robbed, beaten and left for dead by a street gang. People would shout, assuming she was deaf, and push in front of her in queues – and her own self-esteem suffered as she started viewing herself as less important.

This has many features of **ethnography**, such as Moore getting so involved with the experience of the elderly that she came to view herself the way they do. It demonstrates the **commitment** that ethnography can demand – and there are extra ethical issues like **safety** here – but also the insights that come from it. Moore used these experiences in her career as a designer, making appliances to make life easier for the elderly.

METHOD: CONTENT ANALYSIS

So far, we have looked at methods of studying people 'in real life' but sociologists also study the **artifacts** (cultural objects). Artifacts include **media documents** (like books, newspapers, magazines, films, TV programmes and adverts) and **communications** (like diaries, letters, Twitter feeds or transcripts of conversations).

A content analysis involves creating a **schedule** like the schedule used in a **structured observation** (p60, i.e. a checklist). The researcher goes through the artifact counting the number of times certain words, phrases, images or concepts occur. This produces a **quantitative interpretation** (p37) of the artifact. The researcher can also use **semiotics** to carry out a **qualitative interpretation** of the artifact.

Content analyses can **reveal the values and beliefs of the person or culture** that created the artifact. For example, a content analysis of a newspaper reveals our society's preoccupations with sex, violence, money and celebrity. If content analyses span a period of time (i.e, a **longitudinal study**, p36), you can analyse **changing social attitudes** in the rise and fall of certain concepts or images in the media. The artifact can be re-read or re-played many times, making this a very **reliable** method.

Because content analyses don't deal with actual people, there are **no ethical issues** of trust, consent and protection. However, there may be issues of **confidentiality** if you are analysing private communications (such as discussions on social media or private letters).

The main criticisms of content analyses are that they are **subjective interpretations**. For example, a researcher might focus on references to race but not think to look for references to disability or sexuality. This might misinterpret the artifact by over-emphasising something unimportant and missing content that's more important. Similarly, the analysis only reveals **the values and beliefs of whoever created the artifact**, which might not be typical of society. There's a danger when analysing historical artifacts of **imposing modern ideas on the past**, which has **poor validity**.

METHODS PROFILE: MESSNER & COOKY* (2021, cont'd)

Michael Messner & Cheryl Cooky (p37) carried out a **content analysis** of men and women's sports on 3 Los Angeles TV channels and the digital channel ESPN. The researchers recorded 3 two-week segments of sports coverage. The **schedule** included gender of sport (men's, women's, neutral), type of sport (basketball, football, golf, etc.), competitive level of sport (professional, college, high school, etc.) and time given over to the segment (minutes/seconds). **Codes** quantified production values such as music, graphics and game highlights.

It was a **longitudinal study** over 30 years, with an analyses every 5 years. This shows changes from the highly sexualised representation of women's sports in the 1990s to the 'gender-bland' reporting today. It also shows that overall coverage of women's sports has not grown significantly despite calls and pledges to represent more women in sport.

METHOD: STATISTICAL DATA

Statistical data is usually **secondary data** (p30) gathered by non-sociologists but used by sociologists in their research. It is always **quantitative data** (p7) and is particularly valued by Positivists for revealing **social facts**.

- **Official statistics:** This data is gathered by government agencies – in the UK, this usually means the **Office for National Statistics** (**ONS**, *c.f.* p40) and includes data sets with huge samples, like the **UK Census** (p57). Because the government tends to use the same categories and collects data every year, official statistics are a great source of **patterns and trends over time** and can be used in **longitudinal studies** (p36). However, they are subject to **political manipulation** (sometime called 'massaging' the figures) – for example, it might be embarrassing for a government if crime or unemployment goes up, so categories can be redefined to make it look like this isn't happening. For example, raising the school leaving age (ROSLA) reduces unemployment figures.

- **Non-official statistics:** This data is gathered by agencies that aren't the government, such as newspapers, TV shows, charities or market research companies. They tend not to have the enormous **sample sizes** of official statistics and often **don't date back** as far into the past. However, they are **free from political massaging**. The disadvantage is that they can be **methodologically flawed** – for example, people might vote more than once in a newspaper poll or TV phone-in (this is called 'voodoo-polling').

The main advantage of all official statistics is that the data is **easy to access**, often **free** and **up-to-date**.

Interpretivists point out a problem that all statistics are **socially constructed** (*c.f.* Atkinson's criticism of Durkheim, p18). This means statistics do not paint an objective picture of society because they are based on assumptions, definitions and biases by the people who create them. For example, most of us think of unemployment as being out-of-work for any reason, however official government statistics do not count students as unemployed, even though they might be out of work during the long university holidays. Similarly, official crime figures only cover crimes recorded by the police, but lots of crimes are not reported so the real figure is much higher.

AO2 ILLUSTRATION: POLLING COMPANIES

Polling means surveying the public for their views on things. There are several companies that carry out national and international polling.

YouGov in an online polling company based in the UK and founded in 2000. Its surveys usually have samples of 1500-2000 people, but of course its statistics cannot include the views of people who do not have access to the Internet.

Ipsos MORI is another UK polling company based in the UK and dating back to the 1990s. It uses online questionnaires, face-to-face **structured interviews** and computerised telephone surveys.

Gallup and **Pew Research** are American polling companies that carry out worldwide surveys. Pew was founded in the 1990s but Gallup is over a century old. Gallup specialises in gathering data through telephone interviews.

These companies all provide non-official statistics, however on a very large scale. Since they are businesses, their statistics are not always made free to everyone. However Pew Research is a not-for-profit organisation and has a particular focus on reporting religious attitudes.

Research: visit the YouGov FAQ site and investigate the company defends its polling methods from criticism: https://yougov.co.uk/about/panel-methodology/research-qs/

MIXED METHODS: TRIANGULATION

Most research uses more than one method. **Triangulation** means approaching the same social behaviour from two or more angles. It is a way of checking the **validity** (p19) of findings. The results of one method should be backed up by the results of a different method.

- **Internal triangulation** means using different approaches within a single method, such as **open and closed questions** (p56) in a single questionnaire. **Semi-structured interviews** (p58) are a type of internal triangulation.

- **External triangulation** means using two (or more) completely different methods, such as an interview followed by an observation. Interviewing people about their intentions and then observing them to see if they act on those intentions. If they don't do what they said they were going to do, then the interview was **invalid**. The research into care homes by **Gentleman (2009**, p50**)** mixes an observation with interviews.

- **Data triangulation** is when primary and secondary data is combined, such as interviewing people and seeing if their responses match up with the results from official statistics about trends in the country as a whole. The research into social mobility by **Hecht et al (2020**, p30**)** mixes official statistics with Hecht's own interviews with elite earners.

- **Investigator triangulation** is when different observers or interviewers are used, usually from different backgrounds (e.g. different ethnic groups or genders), to see if the social characteristics of the researcher are affecting the respondents or if the researcher's biases are affecting the way they interpret the data.

The main advantage of triangulation is that the **strengths of one method can complement the weaknesses of another**. For example, the big picture from official statistics can make up for the small sample of an interview.

However, triangulation van make research more time consuming and expensive. It does not remove the drawbacks of any of the methods it uses; it just balances them with the strengths of a different one. This is why **Tim May (1993)** states: *"while triangulation might appear attractive, it is not a panacea* [a magical cure] *for methodological ills."*

MIXED METHODS: METHODOLOGICAL PLURALISM

Methodological pluralism is very similar to **triangulation** and the two concepts blur into each other. Triangulation is about checking the validity of research but methodological pluralism is about **deepening and enriching** the data and the conclusions that can be drawn from it.

Case Studies

Case studies are a sociological method that is (weirdly) absent from the OCR Specification, but deserve mention here. Instead of a normal sample group, a case study focuses either on **one unusual individual** or else on **a small group connected by a shared experience** (e.g. a family, a friendship group, people in a workplace, protestors at a demonstration).

This narrow focus can make case studies **hard to generalise** from. However, the advantage is that the researcher can gather **rich in-depth data**. Case studies make use of methodological pluralism to examine the focus individual or group from all angles.

Interpretivists value case studies because you can have immense **empathy** (p15) for the person and view their life history in context. Case studies are often **longitudinal studies** (p36), following a person over a long period of time. However, this intense focus can lead the researcher to become **over-involved** with the person being studied, which is why **reflexivity** is important (p16).

KEY STUDY: WILLIS (1977, cont'd)

Paul Willis' *Learning To Labour* (**1977, p21**) is a case study of 12 working-class 'Lads' that Willis follows through their last year of school and into the workplace.

Willis **observes** the boys in their classrooms and in meetings with their teachers and parents. He **interviews** the boys and their teachers and later their employers. Willis uses this detailed and sympathetic data to question a popular sociological view that working-class boys develop an anti-school subculture because they are frustrated by their lack of success. Willis finds that the boys have no interest in educational success and only want to join the adult workforce.

Willis can be criticised for becoming **over-involved** with the 'Lads': he sometimes seems to excuse their bullying, racist attitudes and destructive impact on other students' learning.

METHODS PROFILE: GENTLEMAN* (2009, cont'd)

Amelia Gentleman spent 4 days observing 26 elderly residents in a care home in Ipswich (p50). She **observes** the residents and **interviews** residents and staff. She paints a distressing picture of the way the elderly are abandoned by their relatives.

Gentleman's 4-day stay is too short for her to become **over-involved** with the residents but perhaps it is also too short for her to build up a deep understanding of what life in the care home is really like (for instance, she does not witness anyone die).

EXAM PRACTICE: THEORY & METHODS

The OCR exam has four questions in **Paper 2 Section A**, based on two source items:

Source A

Views of disabled men & women on how disabled adults are treated compared to non-disabled in the UK

□ Men with disabilities ■ Women with disabilities

YouGov survey of 1008 men and women living with a disability (2018)

Source B

Researchers from the Glasgow Media Group (a group of sociologists linked to Glasgow University) compared and contrasted media coverage of disability in five papers in 2010-11 with a similar period in 2004-5. The papers were *The Sun, The Mirror, The Express, The Mail* and *The Guardian* – including Left and Right Wing political views. The news stories were coded and dominant themes were statistically identified.

They found a significant increase in the reporting of disability (713 articles in 2004-5 compared to 1015 in 2010-11). There was a drop in negative terms like 'cripple' and the presentation of disabled people as victims or sufferers declined. However, there was an increase of reports about disability benefits fraud (2.8% rising to 6.1%) and an increase in negative terms like 'scrounger' and 'skiver' for people on disability benefits (54 examples in 2004-5 going up to 142 in 2010-11).

The researchers recruited focus groups of 6-8 people who were interviewed about their attitudes to disability. They stated that they believed disability fraud was 70% higher than it actually was and cited news articles as evidence for this belief.

Source: *Briant, Watson, & Philo (2011) Bad News for Disabled People: How the Newspapers are Reporting Disability*

1. Summarise the data shown in **Source A**. **[4 marks: 4 AO2]**

*Make **two** points about the data. It is vital that you quote actual figures from the graph and draw conclusions from them (or you are not 'summarising' the data, only restating it). For example, about 46% of women disabilities think disabled adults are treated much worse than other people. In order to summarise, you need to say whether this is higher or lower than males or other opinions.*

2. With reference to **Source B**, explain a strength and a weakness of using triangulation in sociological research. **[6 marks: 2 AO1 + 4 AO2]**

Write a couple of sentences about each evaluation. You might focus on measuring validity, complementary strengths and weaknesses, time & effort and weaknesses still being present – a really good idea is to quote something from the source.

3. With reference to **Source A**, explain **one** advantage and **one** disadvantage of sociologists using non-official statistics as secondary data. **[10 marks: 4 AO2 + 6 AO3]**

*Write two short paragraphs, one about an advantage (such as absence of political massaging) and one about a disadvantage (such as shallowness of statistics, smaller samples, methodology problems). You need to support each reason with an example from the source – a really good idea is to quote a number (or approximate number) from the graph. Make sure that both points link to **non-official statistics**, not just statistics in general.*

4. Using **Source B** and your wider sociological knowledge, explain and evaluate using content analyses to study inequality in society. **[25 marks: 5 AO1 + 5 AO2 + 15 AO3]**

Write four paragraphs/arguments – two strengths and two weaknesses of content analyses would work well. Each paragraph should introduce a sociological idea with an example or comparison from Source B. Each paragraph should finish off with a developed evaluation (see Chapter 4 for this). For example, you could write about content analyses revealing trends over time and wider social values and norms, but also how content analyses only reflect the views of the writers and are limited by the codes the researchers decide to use.

In questions 2-3 you can pick up the AO1 marks from using sociological terminology and relating things to sociological debates (e.g. Positivism vs Interpretivism). Named sociologists and studies aren't particularly important, but knowledge of polling organisations like YouGov is relevant for question 3.

Question 4 is a full essay in which you are invited to deploy *"your wider sociological knowledge"* so famous sociologists definitely belong in your answer and a comparison to other content analyses (like **Messner & Cooky**) or disability research (like **Tom Shakespeare** from **1A: Socialisation, Culture & Identity**) will help.

CHAPTER 4 – EVALUATION

In **Paper 2 Section A**, questions 2, 3 and 4 assess **AO3**/evaluation and only questions 3 and 4 require developed evaluation.

As well as the evaluative points you can find in the preceding chapters, here are some evaluative positions candidates can adopt:

"This is scientific" / Positivism strengths

You can evaluate research for being scientific if it gathers quantitative data, analyses data statistically, uses structured research methods or official statistics, recruits randomised samples and/or studies very large samples and target populations.

Positivism favours scientific research and scientific research has many strengths. It is objective, so it is not interfered with by bias, imagination or wishful thinking. It is evidence-based, which makes it reliable, credible and persuasive. It can predict future trends and patterns, so it is useful for social policy. Since it explains social facts, it can be used to change society for the better, which is also useful for social policy.

To evaluate these ideas, point out examples of scientific research and the influence it has: the way operationalises hard-to-pin-down concepts in measurable ways, the way it can challenge purely anecdotal or personal evidence with a more impersonal view and the way it can offer explanations for things that otherwise look like chance or coincidence.

To elaborate on these ideas, address some flaws in scientific research. It can be narrow and superficial and lacks empathy into what makes people tick. It is often not as objective and value-free as Positivists would like to think. It can view participants as lab rats or guinea-pigs, which leads to ethical issues.

It's important not to be formulaic. Say **why** science is like this: give an example of research and what came out of it. Using ONS data is scientific **because it is drawn from a nationwide sample like the UK Census**. Not all mass surveys are scientific **because they can have unrepresentative samples, such as YouGov ignoring people who don't have Internet access**.

"This is insightful" / Interpretivism strengths

You can evaluate research for being insightful if it gathers qualitative data, analyses data thematically, uses unstructured/naturalistic research methods, uses ethnographic methods and/or studies very small samples and focused target populations.

Interpretivism favours insightful research and Interpretivism has many strengths. It is reflexive, so it addresses its own biases and subjectivity. It explores the social world of ordinary people, so it is generalisable to real life. It uses ethnography to study groups that are often ignored or viewed as deviant. It sees the research participant as important in their own right, so it tends to be ethical and high in validity.

To evaluate these ideas, point out examples of insightful research and the influence it has: the way it encourages case studies, its importance for studying deviant or excluded groups, the way it helps overcome bias and prejudice.

To elaborate on these ideas, address some flaws in Interpretivist research. It can be limited in scope with little to say about society as a whole. It is often subjective and mixes fact and opinion too freely. Is focus on reflexivity can make it wordy with unclear conclusions.

It's important not to be formulaic. Say *why* Interpretivism is like this: give an example of research and what came out of it. Using case studies is insightful *because it challenges stereotypes about the working class, like Willis' study of 'the Lads.'* Not all ethnography is insightful *because researchers can see in cultures only what they want to see, as Freeman criticises Margaret Mead*.

"This describes society" / Structuralism strengths

You can evaluate research for being structuralist (**macro-scale**) if it gathers data about large samples and generalises the findings to society as a whole, discovering patterns and trends.

Structuralism favours large-scale research and large-scale research has many strengths. It is likely to have a representative sample of participants and their behaviour can be generalised to wider society. These conclusions can be expressed statistically and, because they ignore individuals and freewill, they can make predictions about future trends, which is useful for social policy.

To evaluate these ideas, point out examples of structuralist research and the influence it has: the way it dominates official statistics, the influence it has over politicians and voters in elections, its importance for policies like combating crime or unemployment.

To elaborate on these ideas, address the flaw in structuralist research. It ignores the importance of freewill and the social action of individuals or small groups.

It's important not to be formulaic. Say *why* structuralism is like this: give an example of research and what came out of it. Hecht et al's study shows social mobility is reducing *because it draws on data from the UK Census over 40 years*. However, it ignores individual action *because some talented people will still become high earners in spite of this*.

Structuralism is very similar to science/Positivism, and you can often use one to evaluate the other: most scientific studies are also structuralist in scope and outlook; most structuralist research uses scientific procedures. Both share a high respect for statistical data.

"This describes personal relationships" / Social Action strengths

You can evaluate research for being Social Action (**micro-scale**) if it gathers data about small samples and focuses on choice and freewill.

Social Action favours small-scale research and small-scale research has many strengths. It is easier to achieve understanding (**verstehen**) of the participants' social world because you can have empathy and a rapport with them. It is likely to be more ethical because you consider the participants' perspective on things.

To evaluate these ideas, point out examples of Social Action research and the influence it has: the way it sheds lights on groups that are ignored or considered deviant and uses qualitative data to show people resisting social pressures.

To elaborate on these ideas, address the flaw in Social Action research. It exaggerates the importance of freewill and ignores the role that powerful structures like class, race, gender and age play in social behaviour.

It's important not to be formulaic. Say **why** Social Action is like this: give an example of research and what came out of it. Jones et al's study shows people choosing early retirement **because they find it empowering and fulfilling**. However, it ignores social structures **because people from working class backgrounds won't have the option to do this for finabncial reasons**.

Social Action is very similar to insight/Interpretivism and you can often use one to evaluate the other: most Interpretivist studies are also Social Action in scope and outlook; most Social Action research uses Interpretivist procedures. Both share a high respect for qualitative data.

"This is generalisable" / Sampling strengths

You can evaluate research for being generalisable if it is based on representative and/or unbiased sampling.

Representative sampling has many strengths. It is usually stratified (stratified or quota sampling) and draws a large sample group to avoid the risk of unusual participants influencing the findings. Unbiased sampling is usually randomised (random or stratified sampling).

To evaluate these ideas, point out examples of good sampling and the effect it has: the way Positivists can use representative samples to identify patterns and trends in society.

To elaborate on these ideas, address alternative sampling approaches. Sometimes it's important to target a very specific group or a narrow target population that you cannot randomise or no sampling frame exists for (e.g. a criminal gang, homeless people, drug users, illegal immigrants). Sometimes access and gatekeeping force researchers to use a particular sampling technique.

It's important not to be formulaic. Say **why** a particular sample is necessary or undesirable: give an example of research using this sort of sample and how it might be done differently. Willis' sample of schoolboys is not randomised **because he was looking for a very specific group of working class boys with anti-school attitudes**. Hecht et al's purposive sample is justified **because it's difficult to persuade elite earners to take part in research unless you seek them out specially**.

"This is consistent" / Reliability strengths

You can evaluate research for being reliable if it delivers consistent results, has standardised procedures that always work the same way or has been tested with pilot studies or over a long period of time.

Reliable research has many strengths. It is unlikely to be a fluke or one-off result. It can be tested by other researchers or replicated with new samples or in new situations.

To evaluate these ideas, point out examples of reliable research and what makes it so valuable: the standardised procedures that can be followed over and over, longitudinal studies that can test a cohort again and again at regular intervals, clearly operationalised concepts that can be put to use in new situations.

To elaborate on these ideas, address some flaws that make research unreliable. It can focus on a one-off event or unusual groups of people in a situation that will never be repeated. Alternatively, it might have a procedure that is unstructured, so that it never happens the same way twice: unstructured interviews and observations are good examples.

It's important not to be formulaic. Say **why** reliable or unreliable research is like this: give an example of research and how it could be different. Gentleman's research in a care home is unreliable **because she didn't ask standardised questions in her interviews**. Messner & Cooky's content analysis is reliable **because they decided what codes to use and applied the same coding system to different sports TV shows every 5 years**.

"This is unbiased" / Validity strengths

You can evaluate research for being valid if it delivers authentic results, is free from bias or controls in place that prevent interference or distortion of data.

Valid research has many strengths. It is likely to be true and reflects real life. It produces findings that the participants will agree with and other research can confirm.

To evaluate these ideas, point out examples of valid research and what makes it so valuable: the unbiased and value-free stance taken by the researcher, the objective measures being used, techniques like respondent validation and triangulation in use and qualitative data explored in a reflexive way.

To elaborate on these ideas, address some flaws that make research invalid. It can treat statistics in a superficial way. Alternatively, it might have a procedure or sample that is artificial, so that it doesn't reflect real life: structured interviews and observations are can be like this.

It's important not to be formulaic. Say **why** valid or invalid research is like this: give an example of research and how it could be different. Gentleman's research in a care home is valid **because she took an unstructured approach that allowed the residents and staff to express their own views**. Messner & Cooky's content analysis is low in validity **because they focused on a handful of TV shows and ignored sports coverage on radio, in newspapers and on the Internet that might represent women's sports better**.

"This is practical" / Time-cost strengths

You can evaluate research for being practical if it leads to techniques and strategies that can be used by other researchers or the public; in particular, research can have implications for social policy.

Positivism favours practical research and practical research has many strengths. It is credible and persuasive – probably because it has a scientific methodology, a large sample and/or presents statistical data that reveals patterns and trends. However, some research is practical because it has procedures that are cheap and quick to carry out.

To evaluate these ideas, point out examples of practical research and the influence it has: the important sociological concepts and tools that some research introduces or the wide interest by politicians in some sociological ideas.

To elaborate on these ideas, address some flaws in practical research. It can promote social policy that is divisive or destructive; sometimes the data is accused of being politically biased or 'massaged' to suit political agendas.

It's important not to be formulaic. Say **why** practical research is like this: give an example of research and what came out of it. Wilkinson & Pickett's work is practical **because it used official statistics that were already available to show that unequal societies are unhappy**. Not all practical research is beneficial **because Charles Murray's statistical analysis of unemployment in the underclass inspired New Right governments to cut benefits for the poor**.

"This is official" / Official statistics strengths

You can evaluate research for being official if it uses official statistics provided by the government, especially by the Office for National Statistics (ONS).

Official data has many strengths. It has the 'seal of approval' of government statisticians and the ONS is independent from politicians themselves. The data goes back years and is drawn from nationwide surveys like the UK Census. It is available for free through the ONS website.

To evaluate these ideas, point out examples of research using official statistics: the way it can draw attention to patterns and trends affecting the whole country or happening over decades.

To elaborate on these ideas, address some flaws in official data. It can be politically biased or 'massaged' to suit political agendas and its wide scale doesn't suit Interpretivists.

It's important not to be formulaic. Say **why** official data is like this: give an example of research and what came out of it. Hecht's research is official **because it uses the ONS Longitudinal Survey to show social mobility dropping from the 1970s onwards**. Not all official data is trustworthy **because Charles Murray's statistical analysis of unemployment in the underclass is accused of serving a New Right agenda to blame the poor for social problems**.

"This is ethical" / Ethical strengths

You can evaluate research for being ethical if it respects the rights of its participants and preserves the safety of researchers.

There are many ways for research to be ethical. It makes sure that participants give informed consent, are treated honestly, are protected and are guaranteed confidentiality. It ensures the safety of its researchers and doesn't put them in dangerous situations

To evaluate these ideas, point out examples of ethical research and the steps it takes to do the right thing: the way it briefs participants beforehand or explains things to them afterwards, the way it hides true identities and only uses fictitious names and the way it is careful not to break the law.

To elaborate on these ideas, address some problems with ethical research. Sometimes research is ruined if the participants know exactly what it going on or what the researcher is looking for. A certain amount of risk or stress is unavoidable in some real-life situations that sociologists want to study. There are contradictions between keeping your word to participants and reporting crimes to the proper authorities

It's important not to be formulaic. Say **why** ethical research is like this: give an example of research and what came out of it. Willis' study of 'the Lads' is ethical **because he concealed their true names and changed the name of their school to Hammertown Boys School, so as not to ruin its reputation**. Pat Moore's research into old age has ethical problems **because she put herself in danger, as when she was beaten nearly to death by a street gang in New York**.

EXAM PRACTICE: SECTION A

The OCR exam has four questions in **Paper 2 Section A**, based on two source items:

Source A

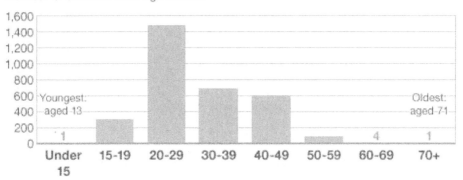

Source: ACPO, 2010

Source B

Geoff Pearson studied football hooligans by carrying out a covert participant observation of Blackpool Football Club supporters between 1995 and 1998. He did this because he had found interviews with supporters to be unreliable, because fans brag about their troublemaking but also hide their worst offences.

The other supporters believed he was a Law student at nearby Lancaster University but did not know he was researching them. Pearson attended 78 games and would meet up with a group of supporters in the pub before or after a match. He did not live in the area, so he could not observe the supporters outside of a football context.

Over time, Pearson became known as a regular fan and he built up a knowledge of the game, the club and the supporters. He found he had to commit 'minor offences' during the research to avoid attracting suspicion. He made a point of only carrying out offences (e.g. pitch invasions) that other supporters did regularly and avoided more serious offences (e.g. violent assaults). Pearson found that his willingness to engage in minor offences gave him the reputation as "*a bit of a nutter*" even though he never took part in anything serious. Nevertheless, he did witness serious assaults.

Pearson concludes that football hooliganism is not 'mindless' and it is not about the violence so much as a sense of community and the excitement of challenging the police.

1. Summarise the data shown in **Source A**. **[4 marks: 4 AO2]**

*Make **two** points about the data. It is vital that you quote actual figures from the graph and draw conclusions from them (or you are not 'summarising' the data, only restating it). For example, 20-29 year-olds receive the most banning orders from football matches, but compare them to other age groups who are similar or very different.*

2. With reference to **Source B**, explain **two** ethical problems with covert participant observations. **[6 marks: 2 AO1 + 4 AO2]**

Write a couple of sentences about each reason. You might focus on deceiving people or the integrity or safety of the researcher. You need to support each reason with an example from the source – a really good idea is to quote something from the source.

3. With reference to **Source A**, explain why respondent validation would be useful to understand this data better. **[10 marks: 4 AO2 + 6 AO3]**

Write two short paragraphs, one about a problem with the validity of the data (such as fans believing they were only bystanders when someone else carried out an offence) and one about how respondent validation could alter the findings. You need to support each reason with an example from the source – a really good idea is to quote a number (or approximate number) from the graph.

4. Using **Source B** and your wider sociological knowledge, explain and evaluate using ethnography to study groups in conflict with the police. **[25 marks: 5 AO1 + 5 AO2 + 15 AO3]**

Write four paragraphs/arguments – two strengths and two weaknesses of ethnography would work well. Each paragraph should introduce a sociological idea with an example or comparison from Source B. Each paragraph should finish off with a developed evaluation (see Chapter 4 for this). For example, you could write about ethnography allowing the researcher to empathise with the group being researched and see through bragging, but also how ethnography tends to be subjective and time consuming.

In questions 2-3 you can pick up the AO1 marks from using sociological terminology and relating things to sociological debates (e.g. Positivism vs Interpretivism, ethical conflicts). Named sociologists and studies aren't particularly important.

Question 4 is a full essay in which you are invited to deploy *"your wider sociological knowledge"* so famous sociologists definitely belong in your answer and a comparison to **Mead**'s ethnography or **Weber**'s theories would also help.

KEY RESEARCH

The studies in this guide are taken from material already presented in **1A: Socialisation, Culture & Identity** or else material that will be introduced in **2B: Understanding Social Inequalities**. The material from 2B is indicated by the * symbol. For each study, I include the key terms, a Perspective (if relevant) and the particular topics it is linked to.

Bourdieu (1984): *Distinction*, cultural capital, habitus; **Positivism**, questionnaire; p22

Correll (2017)*: Small Wins Model; gender equality in work; pilot studies, reflexivity; p32

Durkheim (1897): *Suicide*; comparative method, Functionalism, **Positivism**, statistics; p12

Gentleman (2009)*: study of care home for the elderly; **Interpretivism**, case study, observations, interviews; p50, 52, 59, 61, 67

Hecht et al (2020)*: *Elites Pulling Away*; social mobility, meritocracy; **Mixed Methods**, official statistics, longitudinal, interviews; p30, 34, 35, 37, 39, 45, 47, 59

Jones et al (2010)*: early retirement, quasi-subjects; **Interpretivism**; p35

Martin & Blinder (2020)*: *Biases At The Ballot Box*; racist bias in voting; **Positivist**, questionnaire; p58

McIntosh (1968): *The Homosexual Role*; **Interpretivism**, questionnaires, interviews; p23

Messner & Cooky (2021)*: women in TV sports, longitudinal, quantitative & qualitative; **Positivist**, content analysis; p37, 38, 64

Moore & Conn (1985)*: *Disguised: A True Story*; disguised as 'Old Pat'; **Ethnography**, observation, longitudinal; p63

Murray (1984): *Losing Ground*; unemployment, underclass, New Right; **Positivism**, statistics; p12

Parsons (1959): *The Social Structure of the Family*; gender roles, Functionalism; **Positivism**; p20

Sewell et al. (2021)*: *Commission for Racial & Ethnic Disparities*; social policy, Functionalism; **Positivism**; p27

Weber (1905): *The Protestant Ethic & the Spirit of Capitalism*; Social Action, Interactionism, **Interpretivism**, p18

Wilkinson & Pickett (2009)*: *The Spirit Level*; inequality & happiness, social policy; **Positivism**, statistics; p29, 31

Willis (1977): *Learning to Labour*; social class, education, employment, Marxism; **Ethnography**, observation, case study; p21, 45, 52, 67

FURTHER RESEARCH

These studies are less central to any argument. Some of them just reference a useful piece of terminology or a quote.

Atkinson (1968): *Discovering Suicide*; criticises Durkheim's statistics for being socially constructed, p18

Bryman (1988): problems **with respondent validation**; p34

Comte (1848): coins the terms 'Positivism' and 'Sociology'; p12

Freeman (1983): criticises Mead (1928) p63

Friedan (1963): *The Feminine Mystique*; criticises Parsons' view of gender; p20

Johnson & Duberley (2003): argues **reflexivity** leads to *paralysis*, p18

May (1993): triangulation is not a *"panacea,"* p66

Mead (1935): *Sex & Temperament in Three Primitive Societies*; pioneers ethnography; p61

Williams (2000): three types of **generalisability**; p23

Worsley (1977): defines social problems as causing *"public friction and private misery,"* p39

GLOSSARY

Capitalism: an economic system that promotes the private ownership of property, the pursuit of profit and the concentration of wealth in the hands of a minority of people; the opposite is Communism, which abolishes private property to make everyone economically equal.

Case study: a research tool focusing on a single person, a small group or a single incident; makes use of **methodological pluralism**.

Cohort: the **sample** that takes part in a **longitudinal study**.

Content analysis: a research tool for studying a cultural artifact, which might be a media text or a communication of some sort (e.g. a TV show or a set of letters), for what it reveals about the society that produced it

Cultural Capital: an understanding of high culture that gives you access to the privileges of the wealthy elite, according to **Bourdieu (1984)**

Empathy: having sympathy with and sharing in the emotional states of other people.

Ethnography: a methodological approach taken by **Interpretivists** that involves spending time inside a culture you are studying so as to get a deeper understanding of its members.

Feminism: a sociological Perspective that believes society subordinates women and maintains male power through coercion and violence

Functionalism: a sociological Perspective that promotes consensus around shared values; believes in a biological basis for human social behaviour and a March of Progress that has produced liberal democratic nations as the most successful way of living

Gatekeeping: controlling whether or not researchers can have access to a population they want to study.

Gender: the norms and values linked to biological sex; males are often expected to behave in a masculine way and females in a feminine way: male/female are sexes but masculine/feminine are genders

Generalisability: how a study's findings can be applied to wider society or a **sample**'s behaviour attributed to the target population

Globalisation: a process going on that makes different parts of the world more interconnected through travel, global **Capitalism** and the **Mass Media**; results in the spread of Global Culture and Hybrid Culture but is sometimes resisted

Habitus: your lifestyle and attitudes (including things like dress, accent and values) which place you in a particular social class, according to **Bourdieu (1984)**

Hegemony: the dominance of one group and their culture in society; hegemonic culture is the version of culture that commands the most respect; hegemonic culture might be the culture of the majority of people but it is more often the culture of a wealthy and influential elite

Interactionism: a sociological Perspective that adopts a micro (small scale) approach; believes in understand individual motives and perceptions, often through examining how people play social roles or internalise **labels**

Interpretivism: a methodological Perspective that aims for **empathy** and **rapport** with participants in order to have understanding (***verstehen***) of the meaning of their social world.

Interview: a self-report tool consisting of questions asked out loud that respondents answer by speaking.

Longitudinal: research which takes place over days, weeks or years and measures trends over time.

Marxism: a sociological Perspective that identifies conflict between social classes; believes in a **ruling class** exploiting a **working class**, both through violet force and **ruling class ideology**

Methodological pluralism: using a mixture of methods to create richer and more detailed data.

Neo-Marxism: several new interpretations of **Marxism** that emerged in the 1970s and became mainstream in the 1990s, incorporating elements of **Interactionism** and later **Postmodernism** to traditional Marxist thought

New Right: a sociological Perspective not covered in this book that proposes we are experience social collapse brought on by a welfare culture that rewards worklessness and deviance

Objectivity: Being detached and unbiased; not allowing your values or preferences to influence the research – see **value-freedom.**

Observation: a research tool involving watching participants' behaviour over a period of time

Operationalisation: defining the important concepts in your research in a way that makes it clear how they are being measured

Peer review: a process in scientific reporting where a piece of research has to be checked by other independent scientists before it is published

Pilot study: a small practice version of a study carried out to identify potential roblems

Positivism: a methodological Perspective that aims for scientific standards, **objectivity** and **value-freedom** and the discovery of **social facts.**

Primary data: information the researcher gathers personally

Privilege: the advantages a person has, perhaps without realising it, because they belong to high-status groups or have Identities that are respected in society

Qualitative: expressed in words or descriptions

Quantitative: expressed in numbers or statistics.

Questionnaire: a self-report tool containing written questions that respondents answer in writing.

Rapport: trust and intimacy between researchers and the people they study

Reflexivity: the process of reflecting on the way the researcher influences the people they are studying and vice versa; reflecting about your own biases in research

Reliability: consistency in research; when the research gets the same results every time

Representativeness: how closely the makeup of a **sample** resembles the **target population** it is taken from

Researcher imposition: when the researcher imposes their own views onto the research.

Respondent validation: asking the people who took part in research to evaluate the findings and confirm they agree with them.

Ruling class ideology: a set of beliefs promoted by the ruling class to preserve their power over the working class; ideology hides the injustice in society and justifies it when it cannot hide it

Sample: a small group of people in a study whose behaviour is studied for what it tells you about the **target population** they are taken from

Secondary data: information that already exists because it was gathered by someone else but the researcher makes use of it.

Semiotics: the study of signs and symbols; a technique for interpreting the deeper meaning in **qualitative data**.

Snapshot: the opposite of a **longitudinal study**; research that measures social behaviour at one time and in one situation.

Social class: A system for separating people based on their economic position (wealth, income, status)

Social fact: an underlying rule or law of society that can be used to formulate accurate predictions about social behaviour – a key concept for **Positivism**

Subculture: a group within society that shares some of the **norms and values** of mainstream society but also has distinctive norms and values of its own

Subjectivity: viewing situations from your own unique perspective rather than trying to be detached and unbiased

Target population: the original group the research is investigating from which a **sample** is taken.

Triangulation: using two methods so that the second one can check the **validity** of the first one.

Validity: truth and authenticity in research; when the research shows what the researcher claims it shows

Value-freedom: an **objective** standard for research that is practised by **Positivists**.

Verstehen: A term used by **Max Weber** to mean 'empathic understanding' rather than studying social behaviour in a purely detached and scientific way

ABOUT THE AUTHOR

Jonathan Rowe is a teacher of Religious Studies, Psychology and Sociology at Spalding Grammar School and he creates and maintains **www.psychologywizard.net** and the **www.philosophydungeon.weebly.com** site for Edexcel A-Level Religious Studies. He has worked as an examiner for various Exam Boards but is not affiliated with OCR. This series of books grew out of the resources he created for his students. Jonathan also writes novels and creates resources for his hobby of fantasy wargaming. He likes warm beer and smooth jazz.

Jonathan has created the **Sociology Robot** YouTube channel with video lectures supporting the material in this Study Guide.

Printed in Great Britain
by Amazon

81771675R00047